"I AM WITH YOU"

AUTHOR: PHITO POLYCARPE

Marilyn is a twenty one years old nursing student, with dream of becoming a doctor one day. Marilyn lost her dad to cancer a year ago. Soon after the passing of her dad, her mom's health began to deteriorate.

Marilyn's mom is Mindy. She is the sweetest human being. She is very charismatic, a great mother to her daughter and a wonderful wife to her late husband Colbert April. Since her husband's death she has not been the same. She is recently diagnosed with cancer and has no choice but to quit her job. Since mom is no longer working, Marilyn has no choice but to leave school and get a job to take care of the household. Marilyn and her mom are having a conversation..Let's listen

Mindy: Marilyn..You are still home?..You are going to be late for school..Don't you have school on Tuesdays?

Marilyn: Not anymore mom

Mindy: Your schedule has changed?

Marilyn: No mom..I quit school

Mindy: No..You can't do that..You know what your dad would say about that..You can't do such thing

Marilyn: Mom..If I don't quit school to look for a job..How are we going to survive..You can't work mom

Mindy: Yes I can..Once I started to feel better I will look for a job

Marilyn: Mom..You forgot what the doctor said..You need to rest..The only reason you haven't started the treatment for the cancer is because the doctor said you are too anemic..Once you get a little stronger..You will start the treatment

Mindy: That's just what the doctor thinks..I can't stay here without working

Marilyn: Mom..I will find a job..And everything will be fine..In fact..I have an interview for a job this afternoon

Mindy: What kind of job?

Marilyn: It's at a clinic downtown

Mindy: It's not that bad..It's in the medical field

Marilyn: Mom..It's great..I just need a job..Right now

Mindy: Well..I guess you have to do what you have to do

Marilyn: Mom..I will talk to you later..Call me if you need anything

Mindy: Ok..Good luck baby..Can you please put the medication on the nightstand for me?

Marilyn: Thank you mom..I left the medication on the nightstand and a glass of water as well

Mindy: Thank you..Good luck

Marilyn: Thanks mom..See you later

_At the job place

Marilyn: Good afternoon

Receptionist: Good afternoon..How can I help you?

Marilyn: I am here for a job interview

Receptionist: Ok..At what time is your interview?

Marilyn: It's at three thirty

Receptionist: You are early

Marilyn: Yes..I did not want to be late..I did not know how much traffic I was going to find..There was no traffic at all

Receptionist: You know what they say..Before the time is not the time..After the time is no longer the time

Marilyn: I know..It seems like the exact time is a fine line

Receptionist: It's an eluding fine line..Because the seconds pass really fast..Since you are early..Fill out this application and bring it to me when you are done

Marilyn: Thank you

_A few minutes later

Marilyn: I am done

Receptionist: Ok..Everything seems to be ok..Mrs. Franklin is waiting for you..Second door to your right

Marilyn: Thank you

Receptionist: Good luck

Marilyn: Thank you

Receptionist: Just knock on the door

Mrs. Franklin: Come in

Marilyn: Good afternoon

Mrs. Franklin: Good afternoon..Have a seat please

Marilyn: Thank you

Mrs. Franklin: Was it easy to get here?

Marilyn: Yes..It was..I have a friend who lives not too far from here

Mrs. Franklin: You are familiar with the area

Marilyn: Yes..I am

Mrs. Franklin: These days..Finding a place is very easy..With the help of GPS..Sky views..You can actually visit the area before leaving your home

Marilyn: It is so true..My mom always tells me that my generation is lucky..Everything is easier..She said to find a place..People had to carry a large map

Mrs. Franklin: That's so right..Your mom is right..How did you hear about us?

Marilyn: Online

Mrs. Franklin: I read your resume..And you are in nursing school..Is that correct?

Marilyn: Yes..Well I was..I stop going to school

Mrs. Franklin: You stop going to school?

Marilyn: Yes..I stop..I need to work full time right now

Mrs. Franklin: Well..I would not encourage you to leave school for this job..This is not a job with a lot of growth potential

Marilyn: It's ok..Right now..I desperately need to work..My mom can no longer work..She has cancer..So I have to get a job to support the household

Mrs. Franklin: I am sorry to hear that..I guess you have to do what you have to do..How old are you?

Marilyn: I am twenty one

Mrs. Franklin: May I ask you..Where is your dad?

Marilyn: My dad passed away a year ago..He too had cancer

Mrs. Franklin: I am sorry..I am sorry I did not mean to make you cry

Marilyn: It's ok..I still get emotional when I talk about my dad..He was fine..It happened so quick..Once he found out about the cancer..His healthy started to decline really fast

Mrs. Franklin: I am so sorry..Hopefully one day they will find a cure for cancer

 Marilyn: I hope so

Mrs. Franklin: Since you are in nursing school..You should not have any problem to do this job..Right now..We need someone to work in the admission process of the patients..We are a drug rehabilitation clinic..It's pretty easy..One thing I must mention to you..You will have to deal with body fluids..Such as blood and urine..You know how to draw blood..Right?

Marilyn: Yes I do

Mrs. Franklin: And we encourage our employees to be very careful..Safety first..Because most of the patients have used dirty needles..Many of them are infected with contagious diseases..Employees must wear gloves and eyes shield when dealing with blood

Marilyn: Ok

Mrs. Franklin: You will also have to take the OSHA and HIPPA tests..Also you need to be BLS certified

Marilyn: I took the OSHA and HIPPA tests in school..I am not BLS certified yet

Mrs. Franklin: Don't worry about it..I will send you a link by email..You can take it..We will also pay the fee

Marilyn: Thank you

Mrs. Franklin: You are welcome..You should not have any problem..I really like you..I think you are the right person for the job

Marilyn: Thank you

Mrs. Franklin: In fact..I am not going to interview anyone else..You got the job

Marilyn: Really?..Thank you so much

Mrs. Franklin: You will need to take a drug test within the next twenty four hours..Are you ok with that?

Marilyn: Yes..I am completely fine with it..I don't do drugs

Mrs. Franklin: Good for you..These days..The young people..Most of them use some type of drugs..Last week..We have to fire one young lady because she failed the drug test

Marilyn: So sad

Mrs. Franklin: It is sad..I must tell you that we do random drug testing here..The drug pandemic continues to ravage our communities..So..Marilyn..You get the job..Bring the result of the drug test to human resources tomorrow and they will give you your work schedule and I.D.

Marilyn: Thank you

Mrs. Franklin: Are you available to start right away?

Marilyn: Yes..I am ready..My mom will be very happy..And thank you for the opportunity..I will try my very best to meet the standards of your company

Mrs. Franklin: I know you will..You will do well..It was a pleasure to meet you..I will see you around..Good luck

Marilyn: Thank you

_Marilyn walks out the office..She wipes the tears of joy off her eyes..She knows how much this job means to her..What it means to her mom..A couple years prior..She was just like any other young lady..Happy..Living with both parents..So much happened in her life during this short time..She is in a middle of a storm..She is trying to cope and find a safe place to weather the storm..She lost her dad who was the main source of income in the family..Her mom had a good job..But she can no longer work..Marilyn's mind is racing..She does not want to lose her mom so soon after losing her dad..The tears of joy are soon joined by tears of fears and sadness..Marilyn is a strong young lady..She needs to be strong for her mom..After all they only have each other..She arrives home..She is talking to her mom..Let's listen

Marilyn: Hello mom..How are you feeling?

Mindy: I am fine baby..How was the interview?

Marilyn: It went fine

Mindy: I took a little nap..I dreamed that you get the job

Marilyn: Really? Your dream came true

Mindy: What do you mean?

Marilyn: I got the job

Mindy: Really? On the spot

Marilyn: Yes

Mindy: They must have been nice people..I didn't think you were ready to interview for a job

Marilyn: Mom..You need to give me credit..You still think that I am a baby

Mindy: You will always be my baby

Marilyn: I am your grown baby mom..I am a lady mom..Are you surprised of the news?

Mindy: What news?

Marilyn: Of the news that I am a lady

Mindy: I am..Because just the other day I was changing your pamper

Marilyn: Very funny mom..I see you kept your sense of humor through it all..Those days are long gone mom..The only pamper you should think of changing now is your grandchild's..You will soon have some grand children

Mindy: Really? Don't be in a rush for that..Focus on your career first

Marilyn: I know..I know mom..I am only kidding..I am not ready to have kids any time soon..I am going to prepare dinner..What do you want to eat mom?

Mindy: I don't have appetite baby..I can't tell you..You make whatever you want

Marilyn: Mom..You remember what the doctor said..You need to eat in order to become stronger..The sooner you start the treatment the better

Mindy: I know..I know..Since your dad passed away..My will to live has decreased..He was my best friend

Marilyn: Mom..Don't be so selfish..What about me..I want you to live..You want me to be left alone in this world

Mindy: I know baby..Of course not..I don't want you to be left alone..But your dad was everything to me

Marilyn: I know mom..I miss him too..But now it is time to fight for your life..That's what dad would like you to do

Mindy: I understand..But it is so difficult when you live with someone for so long..And all of a sudden he is gone..Everything happens at once..Now I have cancer..I can't work to support you

Marilyn: Mom..You don't have to worry about supporting me..I am twenty one years old..I am a big girl now

Mindy: You did not have to quit school..I feel bad about that

Marilyn: Mom..Worry does not solve anything..Only actions will solve a problem..I am going to work..You will beat the cancer and everything will be fine..That's the mindset you must have

Mindy: I am so proud of you..I did not know you were that strong

Marilyn: It's up to you if you still want to think of me as a baby..I am a grown woman

Mindy: You are not that grown

Marilyn: I know what you are going to say next.Just the other day you were changing my pamper

Mindy: You read my mind

Marilyn: You are so funny mom

_A couple of hours later

Marilyn: Mom..Dinner is ready..You want me to bring your dinner in the bedroom for you?..Mom..Mom..Why you are not answering me?..Mom?

Mindy: Hi

Marilyn: Mom..You scared me..I've been calling you and you did not answer me

Mindy: I am sorry baby..I did not mean to scare you

Marilyn: I thought something happened to you

Mindy: You thought I was dead?

Marilyn: I just thought you passed out

Mindy: Baby..Dying is part of life..We all have to go at some point

Marilyn: Mom..I don't want to hear that..I am not ready for that yet..I don't want you to leave..This is not your time yet..I want you to fight this illness..I will help you fight it..I will do whatever I can mom..It is s not right..I just lost dad..That's about the most pain I can handle

Mindy: Baby..Baby..No need to get upset..I am here..I am not dead

Marilyn: I know mom..But I need you to gather your will to fight..I can't afford to lose you

Mindy: Baby..You have to be strong..Anything is possible..I may die..But..Time heals all

Marilyn: Not so true..It has been a year since dad passed away..But time has not yet healed my pain mom

Mindy: Well..Honey some pains require more time for the healing

Marilyn: Well..In this case it will take a life for the healing..Mom..Would you fight please?

Mindy: Baby..Of course I will fight..What are you talking about..You think I want to leave you alone in this world?

Marilyn: It is not only about me..I think you deserve to live a longer life mom..You have more things to see..More places to visit..More people to meet

Mindy: More food to taste if only I could have dinner

Marilyn: This is the mom I want..The one with the sharp sense of humor..Yu want to eat here in your room or you want to eat on the table?

Mindy: I want to eat at the table..I've been in bed all day..I need to get up a little

Marilyn: I concur..So let's go mom..I made something you will enjoy

Mindy: What is it?

Marilyn: I can't tell you..It's a secret

Mindy: It's going to be the shortest secret ever..I am on my way to the table..A couple steps secret?

Marilyn: Whatever mom..Where did you get your sense of humor mom? Is it from grandma or grandpa?

Mindy: Grandma?..Not at all..Grandma was very serious..She did not play at all..Dad was the one with the humor..He would say..I try to keep her laughing so she does not murder you baby..My mom did not play at all..Everything was a serious business to her..But..There was balance because my dad did not take himself serious at all

Marilyn: OK..I thought grandma was the funny one..Mom..Eat..I did not give you much

Mindy: The food is pretty good..I would love to eat a lot but I don't have appetite

Marilyn: Try the salad mom..I don't want you to leave so soon

Mindy: Well..Just a few minutes ago you were telling me that you are so grown up..Now you dropping a box of pampers on my lap

Marilyn: The box of pamper is for the your grandchildren

Mindy: I don't want to hear it

Marilyn: Get some shake mom..It's a protein shake..It's good for you..Did you take your vitamins today?

Mindy: Yes I did..I feel good

Marilyn: You will start to feel better soon..Just keep eating and take your vitamins..You will beat this cancer mom

Mindy: I hope so..I started to feel a little sick..Feel like vomiting

Marilyn: Well..Just go lay down mom..My phone is ringing

Marilyn: Hello

Nora: Hello..Marilyn..How are you?

Marilyn: I am fine Nora

Nora: Nathalie told me that you stop going to school this semester

Marilyn: She told you that?..I am going to kill her

Nora: Was it supposed to be a secret?

Marilyn: Not at all..But..I wanted to tell people myself

Nora: I don't see the big deal..I asked her about you and she said you are not in school this semester..Why though?

Marilyn: I have some urgent obligations that I need to take care of

Nora: Like what?

Marilyn: My mom is no longer working

Nora: I am sorry..I did not know she lost her job

Marilyn: She did not lose her job..She had to stop working due to her health condition

Nora: What is wrong?

Marilyn: She has breast cancer

Nora: Oh god..I did not know that..When did she find out about it?

Marilyn: It's been three weeks now..She will start chemo therapy soon

Nora: I am so sorry..I will come see her tomorrow..Be strong Marilyn..She will be fine..Have you found a job yet..If not..You could go to Robert's job..They are hiring now

Marilyn: I found one..I had an interview yesterday

Nora: But you are not sure whether you are going to get it..Sometimes people don't call back after the interview

Marilyn: I know..But..She hired me on the spot

Nora: That's wonderful..I will stop by tomorrow

Marilyn: I work tomorrow..I start training tomorrow..Mom will be here..You can always pass by and see her

Nora: I will wait and come when you are there..At what time you get off work?

Marilyn: I should be home by five

Nora: Ok..I will come by six o'clock

Marilyn: Ok Nora..See you tomorrow

Nora: Say hello to her for me

_The next day at the Marilyn's job

Marilyn: Good morning

Mrs. Franklin: Good morning Marilyn..Are you ready to start?

Marilyn: Yes I am

Mrs. Franklin: Come with me..I need to introduce you to Julie..She will be training you..Here is where you will find your mask and gloves..This is a wash station just in case you get splashed with blood..You come here to wash your face and your eyes

Marilyn: That has happened before?

Mrs. Franklin: Yes..In fact to me..Not at this place..At my previous job..We were doing an Fgram for a patient..We were going retrograde and somehow the wire got out and I got splashed with blood

Marilyn: What did you do?

Mrs. Franklin: I did not have eyes guard on..But I had my glasses on..I broke scrub and ran to the station..Luckily I knew where the station was..They drew blood from the patient to conduct tests..She was HIV and Hip negative..Another time..We were inserting a port for a patient and I got stuck by a needle..Luckily the needle was a clean one..You have to be very careful

Marilyn: Can you do that..Test the patient for HIV?

Mrs. Franklin: This is an OSHA requirement..The patient has to sign the consent form..In case of an incident involving blood..Patient will be tested for those diseases

Marilyn: I did not know that

Mrs. Franklin: I did not know everything either..But remember safety first..This is Julie..And Julie this Marilyn

Marilyn: You said that you were inserting a port for a patient..What is a port

Mrs. Franklin: A port is a device we put in the patient chest..Not too deep..Just below the epidermis..Usually for patient who are undergoing chemo therapy

Marilyn: My mom might need one..What does it do?

Mrs. Franklin: It is used for the treatment..To prevent the patient from being stuck at a different place every time..They know where the port is..They can feel it under the patient's skin..They inject the chemo treatment there..The port has a small tube that is fed into the patient's subclavian..It is similar to a line put in the patient's neck or chest for dialysis treatment

Marilyn: Wow..I learned so much already..Inserting a port is a long process?

Mrs. Franklin: Not at all..It all depends on the surgeon..It's pretty simple..Me..It used to take me..The most..I would say ten minute to insert a port..Once the patient has been sedated and preps..I inserted the needle to into the IJ..Some surgeons prefer the subclavian..Me..I prefer the IJ..Once the needle is in..I have blood coming out..I insert the guide wire..Then I put the sheath over the wire

Marilyn: what is the sheath?

Mrs. Franklin: The sheath is a very tiny trocar..It's a device that holds a spot open..Trocars are used in laparoscopic surgeries..Usually into the peritoneal cavity..From which the cameras and surgical tools are inserted..Once the sheath is in..I mark the spot on the patient's chest for the incision..After the incision..I create a pocket for the port..I insert the port into the pocket..Then I use the tunneler to tunnel the line or tube toward the sheath..Cut the tunneler away..Then I insert the line inside the sheath..Make sure the line or tube is well inside the IJ..Then I split the sheath..I take picture to make sure the line is well placed..Then I close the incisions with monocryl and vicryl ..Put the dressings on and it is done

Marilyn: You made it sound so easy

Mrs. Franklin: For some hospital inserting a port or catheter is a very complicated procedure..Not for me

Marilyn: I did not know you were a doctor?

Mrs. Franklin: Yes I am..I am in charge of this clinic now..I have not been inside an O.R. in years

Marilyn: You still sound sharp

Mrs. Franklin: Well..Not as sharp as a number fifteen scalper..This is Julie..Hello Julie

Julie: Hello..Hello

Mrs. Franklin: Julie..This is Marilyn

Julie: Hello Marilyn

Marilyn: Hello Julie

Mrs. Franklin: Basically..Marilyn will shadow you for a couple of weeks..I think after two weeks she should be ok

Julie: I think so..Usually it only takes two weeks for them to become expert

Mrs. Franklin: I don't know about expert..But we want her to be ready..Ok ladies..Become best friends..Do you have any question for me?

Marilyn: Can I keep my phone on me..Just in case my mom calls me

Mrs. Franklin: Yes you can..But..You don't want to contaminate your phone..I you are wearing dirty gloves..Don't grab your phone..Have someone else whose hands are not contaminated to reach in your pocket and get it for you..Safety first

Marilyn: Thank you

Mrs. Franklin: Don't forget to take your lunch..I f you take it..It's your loss..They will deduct thirty minutes from your time anyway..Just go to lunch when Julie is going

Marilyn: Thank you

Julie: I will take care of her..She will be fine

_Later that day

Mindy: How was your day?..I cooked something

Marilyn: Mom you need to rest..You don't have to cook for me

Mindy: I feel much better today..So I went to the kitchen and cooked something

Marilyn: You don't have to do that mom

Mindy: You prefer that I stay in bed all day?

Marilyn: No..Not staying in bed all day..But at the same time..I don't want you to try to do too much too soon

Mindy: I am feeling pretty good..I started to get my strength back..Who's at the door?..Someone rang the bell honey

Marilyn: I know mom..It's Nora..She told me that she will pass by

Karl: Hi

Marilyn: Karl..What are you doing here?

Karl: You expected someone else? You expected another guy?..Sorry about your disappointment

Marilyn: C'mon..Don't be ridiculous..My friend Nora supposed to stop by..I thought it was her at the door

Karl: I come here because you are not answering my calls..I texted you twice today..You did not answer..I learned that you stopped going to school from one of your friends

Marilyn: You are not my dad..I don't have to tell you or ask you for permission regarding my every decision

Karl: I know I am not your dad..But last time I checked..We were together

Marilyn: Right..We are together when we are together..That's about it

Karl: What do you mean?

Marilyn: We are seeing each other..There is no commitment between us..And it's only been two months since I know you..You should not expect me to tell you everything that is going on in my life

Karl: Is that right? I think in a relationship..One should not have any secrets

Marilyn: Karl..I am sorry those were things I did not feel comfortable to discuss with you

Karl: I understand that..But if you are going to quit school I think I should know about that

Marilyn: What this has to do with you

Mindy: Marilyn..Is this Nora?

Marilyn: No mom..It's Karl

Karl: Hello Mrs. Blackwood

Mindy: Hello Karl..How are you?

Karl: Fine..Thank you..How are you?

Mindy: I haven't been feeling too well lately..But today was a good day..You look different

Karl: I had a haircut

Mindy: Nice to see you

Karl: Yes..To get back to the subject..You can't quit school

Marilyn: What do you mean?..I already did..Besides..It is none of your business

Karl: There is no reason in the world that will justify you quitting school in my world

Marilyn: Karl..I am not trying to justify anything for your world

Karl: I will tell you straight up..If you are not going to school..We cannot be together

Marilyn: I made the decision based on a very important situation..Quitting school was part of my obligations..And another aspect of my obligations right now is to show you the door

Karl: What do you mean?

Marilyn: Walk you out of my house..Simple as that

Karl: Really?

Marilyn: Yes..Really..Bye Karl..It was nice to know you

Karl: I knew you were up to something..Your silence for the last few weeks told me that you were with someone else

Marilyn: Yes..I am with someone..I am with my mom..At this time..She needs all of me in other to win her battle against cancer

Karl: She has cancer?

Marilyn: Bye Karl..Don't let the door hit you

Mindy: Karl left already?

Marilyn: Yes mom..He is gone..My phone is ringing..Where is it?

Mindy: You left it right here in the room

Marilyn: Where mom

Mindy: On my nightstand

Marilyn: Hello

Nora: Hello

Marilyn: Where are you?

Nora: I am right around the corner from your house..I am calling to ask you whether you want something to eat

Marilyn: No thank you Nora..I cooked dinner..Don't buy anything..I have food here

Nora: You cooked..I did not know you can cook?

Marilyn: You have a lot to learn about me sister

Nora: Can't wait to taste that food

Marilyn: Nora..What are you saying?..Didn't I cook that time we went camping?

Nora: Yeah..You are right..You made spaghetti

Marilyn: Not just spaghetti..Don't be a hater Nora

Nora: I am not a hater..You want to kill me because I forget about the sauce

Marilyn: You purposely forgot about it

Nora: Not really..Don't be so sensitive

Marilyn: Where are you?

Nora: Hold your horse's lady..I am pulling in your driveway right now

Marilyn: I see you..I did not know you had a green car?

Nora: That's my mom's..Mine is at the shop

Marilyn: What is wrong with it?

Nora: Why are we on the phone still..We are right in front of each other

Marilyn: I know right

Nora: Nothing is wrong..Just for oil change..What have you been up to miss quitting school?

Marilyn: My life is upside down..You remember those days when I used to be so happy

Nora: You haven't been the same since your dad passed away

Marilyn: I thought by now..I would have shaken the pain off..But obviously not

Nora: Marilyn..In order to shake the pain off..You must be willing to let go

Marilyn: I tried..It seems that this is something I will live with for the rest of my life..Now..My mom is sick

Nora: Where is your mom?..I want to say hello to her

Marilyn: Mom..Mom..Nora is here..She wants to say hello to you

Mindy: I am getting dressed..I will be out soon

Marilyn: She just took a shower

Nora: How is she doing mentally?

Marilyn: She is doing pretty well..She still maintains her sense of humor..She makes me laugh every day..I don't know how I will be able to go on if I lose her

Nora: Don't talk that way..She will be fine

Marilyn: It is hoping for the best and be prepared for the worst

Nora: I know..I know

Mindy: Where is Nora..Hello Nora..How are you my dear?

Nora: I am fine..How are you?

Mindy: I am ok..The evil cancer is trying to remove me from this world

Nora: I heard..But..I think you will win the battle..What kind of treatment method you will consider?

Mindy: It is going to be chemo

Marilyn: This is a very aggressive carcinoma cell..Therefore the doctor recommended chemo as the treatment approach

Nora: Are you ready to lose your beautiful hair?

Mindy: It does not matter to me..Better the hair than my life

Marilyn: Once she starts to lose her hair..I will shave mine as well

Mindy: No you don't have to do that baby

Marilyn: Just as a form of support mom..You don't feel different

Nora: That's nice..Maybe I should join you and shave mine too

Mindy: Guys..Don't do it..I will be fine..Karl might not like it..Some men don't like women with short hair

Marilyn: Mom..First of all I am not my hair..Second..I don't have any Karl in my life

Mindy: I am not my hair is a song..Do you know that?

Marilyn: Really?

Nora: Of course..India Arie wrote that song

Marilyn: Of course..Of course..What was I thinking?

Mindy: Did you say that you don't have a Karl in your life..Am I dreaming..Wasn't it Karl that was here a few minutes ago?

Marilyn: Mom..This is the past..Was..Emphasis on was

Nora: What happened between you and Karl..I thought everything was ok?

Marilyn: Not anymore..I don't think he is mature enough to understand my situation..What I have to deal with

Nora: Really?..What did he say or do?

Marilyn: He said that he can't be with me if I am not in school..This is no time to explain myself trying to make a dude understand me..I lost my dad not too long ago..I am trying not to lose my mom..This is no time for me to kiss a man's feet..So I showed him the door

Mindy: Marilyn always had a temper since she was a little girl

Marilyn: Mom..It is not about my temper..I was not even upset..It's a decision I made calmly..He needed to go..Because..To tell you the truth I have no time for that..My mind is wrapped around my mom's illness right now..I need no other distraction..What I am dealing with now is all that I can take

Nora: I hear you

Mindy: When did the argument occur..I did not hear anything

Marilyn: Mom..There was no argument

Nora: So..I got up and walked away..Without saying anything

Marilyn: Well..He did not have to get up..He was already standing..Karl knows me pretty well..He knows when I said get out I mean it..He knows I am not the type that goes back to decision that I made regarding breaking up with a guy..I told him my story with Sidney

Nora: I forgot..Why did you break up with Sidney?

Marilyn: He was supposed to come to my house..And he said he could not come..And I told him stay home and don't come back

Nora: Oh my god Marilyn..This is not right..You should have given him another chance

Marilyn: You have to understand..This is not the first time he told that he would come to my house and did not show up..That day I had enough..Besides..My mom had invited me to go to the movies..I said no thinking Sidney was coming..When he said he could not come..I shot it down

Nora: You shoot from the hip

Marilyn: Quick and sharp too..Do you want to eat?..You don't seem hungry..Maybe..You are not that interested

Nora: C'mon Marilyn..What are you saying..You are a much better cook than I am

Marilyn: Really?

Nora: I don't cook..I only buy food from restaurants..This is not good

Marilyn: How come you are not fat..You seem to be in shape

Nora: I am not fat..But not in the best shape either..I could look better..My behind is too big

Marilyn: Are you kidding me? You look good in those jeans

Nora: I want it to be a little firmer

Marilyn: You are fine..This is not the time to start your diet..I have made spaghetti with ham and shrimp..And also freshly baked biscuits

Nora: Oh my god..If I come here too often I will be fat..The sauce tastes so good

Marilyn: This is an oyster sauce

Nora: You made it from scratch

Marilyn: I would love to get the credit..But..I bought it from the store..Then I put different spices in it..I enhanced the taste

Nora: You should get the credit..I bought oyster sauces before from the store..They never tasted that good..I think it's the spices you put in there that gave it such a wonderful taste

Mindy: I am very impressed about her cooking

Marilyn: This means a lot to me coming from you mom

Mindy: Really? Why is that?

Marilyn: Well..You never gave me credit from anything

Mindy: I am sorry my dear..You are the best

Marilyn: Whatever mom..I know you don't mean it

Nora: She does

Marilyn: Nora..You have no idea..My mom always tells me..Just the other day I was changing your pampers

Mindy: It just means that the time passed so fast

Marilyn: No mom..It means you think I am a baby..I can't do anything

Mindy: Not at all..You get it all wrong baby..Mommy believes in you

Marilyn: Whatever

Mindy: Nora..It was nice seeing you..I am going in to lay down a bit..And I don't want to miss my show

Nora: What show is that?

Marilyn: Dancing with the stars

Mindy: No..Not that..The bachelor..The finale is tonight

Marilyn: How could you love a show such as that?

Mindy: What's wrong with it?

Marilyn: Mom..You don't see what is wrong with it?..You have a bunch of women competing for one guy..He goes out with one of them every day..Kissing each and every one..What kind of trash is that?..Even if that guy was the last left on this planet I would not be amongst those women

Nora: Really? I never watched it

Mindy: It's just a show Marilyn..It is not that serious

Marilyn: Mom..It is that serious..Some of the girls are crying for him when he goes out with other women..They are waiting for him to come back for a chance to kiss him too..Nasty

Mindy: Marilyn..Enough..It's just a show..I don't look at all these details..I don't give it that much thought..I just want to see who is going to win..Who he is going to pick

Marilyn: Well..As a young lady..I think it is degrading for women

Mindy: Degrading if you are participating in the show..You can watch the show

Nora: I think your mom has a point..You would never be a cast member..But you can watch it ..Just to see who has the best game amongst those women

Mindy: I think you should watch it baby..You could improve your game about how to get a man

Marilyn: Thank you mom..But no thank you..My man would not go out with three women while I am waiting for him to come back to get a kiss

Nora: It's just a show Marilyn

Marilyn: Not for me

Nora: The food was delicious

Marilyn: Thank you..If you want I can give some to bring home with you

Nora: No..I am fine..You really want me to get fat..Don't you?

Marilyn: Tomorrow..I will bring some to work to eat at lunch time

Nora: How is the job?..You like it?

Marilyn: It's ok..There is a little dangerous aspect to it..Because you are dealing with patients who are drug addicts..Some of them are infected with contagious diseases..But..It is challenging..And I feel that I am making a difference by helping those people

Nora: So..It is rewarding?

Marilyn: Yes..I can say that

Nora: What is your schedule?..You work every day?

Marilyn: Monday through Friday

Nora: You are off on weekend..We can hang out one weekend

Marilyn: Not any time soon..My mind is all wrapped around that cancer..I am not a mood to hang out now

Nora: I understand..I will stop by more often to see how you are doing..It is getting late..You are working tomorrow..So I have to go to let you rest

Marilyn: You are working tomorrow..Right?

Nora: No..I am off tomorrow..But I a lot of stuff to do

Marilyn: The usual stuff..Do your nails..Your hair

Nora: Those too..But I have some other stuff to do..I will see you in a couple of days..Your mom might be sleeping

Marilyn: Mom..Mom..I think she is sleeping

Nora: Tell her I said goodbye

Marilyn: I sure will..Thank you for coming Nora..For years..You remain a good friend..A sister to me

Nora: A sister from another mother..See you..Take care

_The next day at the work place

Mrs. Franklin: Hello Marilyn..Let me introduce you to our newest member..This is Gary

Marilyn: Hello Gary..Nice to meet you

Gary: Nice to meet you

Mrs. Franklin: You guys will be working together most of the time..Gary is medical school student

Marilyn: Oh..Really?

Gary: I can use this work as credits toward my degree

Marilyn: Very good

Mrs. Franklin: I will leave you guys..Get to know each other..I will see you later..I am having a staff meeting at two o'clock..I would appreciate it if both of you could be there

Marilyn: I will be there

Gary: I will be there...At two right?

Mrs. Franklin: Yes at two o'clock..See you guys there

Gary: How do you like the job?

Marilyn: I think it's ok..It's just a job..Not so bad..Those people are drug addicts..They do need help

Gary: I see..What where you doing before this job?

Marilyn: I was in nursing school

Gary: Which one? My teaches at the one on Marcy Ave

Marilyn: That's the one I was attending

Gary: Do you still go?

Marilyn: I feel like I am having a second interview for this job

Gary: Sorry..If I make you feel this way

Marilyn: I feel like I was being interrogated by the FBI or something

Gary: Not at all..I am just trying to know you..You don't ask me any questions because you are not interested in who I am

Marilyn: You are probably wrong

Gary: Wrong regarding what?

Marilyn: About I am not interested in knowing who you are

Gary: Well..You did not even ask me one question

Marilyn: If you had given me the chance..I could have asked you a question or two..But your interrogation was so aggressive..I did not have a chance..I manage to find out that your mom works at the nursing school

Gary: I provided that information to you without you asking..You were born here?

Marilyn: Here we go

Gary: Ok..Ok I will stop talking

Marilyn: I am kidding..Yes I was born and raised here..And you?

Gary: I moved here when I was sixteen..I went to high school here

Marilyn: Which High school did you attend?

Gary: Saint Alpine High

Marilyn: You went to private school..You are a rich brat

Gary: Not really?..My mom did not care about us going to public school..But my dad wanted us to go to private school

Marilyn: That was the opposite for me..My dad..Although he could afford it..He wanted me to go to public school..I enjoyed it though..I don't think there was anything wrong with it..I made great friends..To this day my best friends are from my school

Gary: I would not have minded it either..But my dad wanted to do it

Marilyn: What does he do?

Gary: He is a U.S. Senator

Marilyn: Ok..You like politics?..You will follow on your dad footsteps?

Gary: Not at all..I really love the medical field

Marilyn: People get into politics after becoming doctors

Gary: You are right..There were two doctors amongst the republican candidates..Doctor Ben Carson..And what is the other guy's name?

Marilyn: I believe it is Cruz

Gary: I think so

Marilyn: Here are your precedents..You will run for office just like your father

Gary: No..I am sure about that..What do you want to do later?

Marilyn: My goal is to become a doctor as well..But right now things are not looking too bright

Gary: You have time..Some people have children before starting medical school..Talking about children how many you would like to have?

Marilyn: Me..Maybe one if any at all

Gary: I am disappointed..I want three kids

Marilyn: You are disappointed?..Excuse me..You can go ahead and have your three kids..What are you disappointed about Gary?

Gary: You said you only want one child

Marilyn: Are you looking for a surrogate mother?..I can't help you

Gary: I was hoping you could have my children

Marilyn: You are so funny Gary..You know that..Funny and bold

Gary: How so?

Marilyn: How so?..I only met you a few minutes ago..And you are already planning to get me pregnant

Gary: C'mon..Don't put words in my mouth..I never said I wanted to get you pregnant

Mrs. Franklin: Who is pregnant?..Are you pregnant Marilyn?

Marilyn: No..Not at all..I don't think I will ever be..I am not too crazy about having children

Mrs. Franklin: I was the same way..I had my first child when I was thirty five..And my son was born two years after

Marilyn: I am not too crazy about having children..My friend Michelle had her first child when she was in high school..I saw how difficult it was for her..So..I said to myself..I am not having any until I am fully ready

Mrs. Franklin: You guys have gotten acquainted?

Marilyn: Too much..I think he is a little too comfortable

Mrs. Franklin: Really?

Gary: I don't know what getting too comfortable means?..Is it a good or bad thing?

Marilyn: It's a good thing..He is very open..Not shy at all..I think he will do well with the patients

Gary: Thank you

Mrs. Franklin: It's very good to hear Gary

Gary: Especially from a senior employee such as Marilyn..There is no better acknowledgment

Marilyn: Very funny Gary

Mrs. Franklin: She has two whole days of seniority

Marilyn: Yeah right..See how great a sense of humor he has?

Mrs. Franklin: I see that

Marilyn: Too bad he is in the wrong place..He misses his vocation..Nobody needs a funny doctor at their bedside

Gary: I do

Marilyn: I don't..I want a very serious doctor at my bedside

Gary: Somebody like doctor Kevorkian

Marilyn: Who is that?

Gary: The death doctor..You don't remember the doctor who was helping people committing suicide?

Marilyn: Yes..Yes I remember him..Well..Not as serious as doctor kervokian

_Through the weeks and months Marilyn and Gary had developed a strong friendship..They go to lunch together every day..They exchange food in many occasions..Gary loves Marilyn cooking..It is a pleasure for her to bring him different dishes..Gary occasionally brings her some cookies that his mother bakes..Every Friday they go out for lunch..One Friday Gary invites Marilyn out for dinner..Let's listen:

Marilyn: Thank you for the lunch..I really appreciate your kindness..You are a gentleman..But I will stop going out to lunch with you

Gary: Why would you do such thing..This is my favorite time of the day..Spending time with you means a lot to me

Marilyn: Gary..You really know how to make a woman melt with your words..I will stop going out at lunch time with you because you don't let me pay..Not once..This is not good..I want to pay for your lunch..Let me do it at least once..You pay every time for me

Gary: This is the reason you are not going out to lunch with me anymore?

Marilyn: Yes..How do you think I feel when you pay for my lunch every time...And you don't let me pay once for you

Gary: I thought that's what women love

Marilyn: Not at all..I am not that kind of woman..I know some women just like to receive gifts..Favors..Dinner..You name it..Everything from men and never offer anything..Not even once..I think it's really bad

Gary: Well..I think you passed the test..I was just testing to see how selfish you are..You are a wonderful person..Some women are in fact very selfish..They love to receive and don't show any reciprocity..I think it's very ugly and show a lot about the personality of that person..I don't mind spending for someone I love..I will give you the world..But if I realize that you are a selfish person who only cares of receiving..To me it is the biggest turn off

Marilyn: Not only a turn off..It is an ugly thing..So..You were testing me?

Gary: I was testing to see how long you will let me treat you without offering to do the same

Marilyn: I am not that kind of woman..Why would I try to get as much as I can from a man with no reciprocity..I think in any relationship..Friendship there should be no room for selfishness

Gary: I don't think a person who is very selfish can rally love others

Marilyn: So I passed the test?

Gary: Yes you did

Marilyn: I was saying to myself..What is wrong with this guy..I was about to just stop going out with you for lunch

Gary: Really?

Marilyn: That's how strong I felt about it..Even though we are friends..I was feeling very uncomfortable with you buying me stuff every time

Gary: Who says we are friends?

Marilyn: Excuse me?

Gary: I don't spend that much money on lunch for any of my friend

Marilyn: Very funny Gary..Last time I checked we were still friends

Gary: Not me..Last time I checked you were the woman of my dreams..The one I want to have children with

Marilyn: Gary..Gary..What are you saying..You joke too much

Gary: I am not joking Marilyn..You are the reason I get up early every morning to come here

Marilyn: C'mon..I won't buy this from you Mr. smooth talker..You wake up early every morning because you don't want to get fired from your job..Not for me

Gary: You are so wrong..I have no need to work..My dad opposes to it..I have already accumulated the hours necessary for my medical school credits..The only reason I am still working here it's because of you

Marilyn: Really?

Gary: I come here every day for a chance to see you..For a chance to be next to you..For a chance to hear your voice..I come here every day Marilyn..For a chance to see you smile..I know you might not believe me..But..Right now it is not me talking..It is a pale translation of how my heart is feeling about you

Marilyn: Gary..Gary..You are making me blush..I don't know what to say..I like you..You are a nice guy..A gentleman..But I did not expect you to talk in such way about me..About us..I did not know you were feeling this way about me

Gary: Well..Marilyn..Now you know..I just wanted to let you know that we have been husband and wife for a long time

Marilyn: Very funny..I am the only one who did not know about it

Gary: Well..It was not easy for me to let you into our romance..I am happy that now you know..How do you feel about the information?

Marilyn: What information Gary?

Gary: The fact that we have been husband and wife

Marilyn: You are too funny..I don't see any ring in my finger..How could we be husband and wife?

Gary: We have imaginary rings

Marilyn: All I can say..Next time you decide to make us husband and wife..I would appreciate it if you let me be part of it

Gary: This is a promise I make to you..From this day forward you will be part of everything that I am doing..And I will certainly do a proper demand for your hands..Can we conclude this conversation with a nice kiss and look forward to becoming husband and wife

Marilyn: Oh my god..This guy is too much..What do you mean by nice kiss?

Gary: Well..I can show you better than I can explain it..Come closer to me

Marilyn: Oh my god..Gary you are going to get me fired

Gary: Why you wiped your lips?

Marilyn: You wet my lips..You are a messy kisser

Gary: You think so..You did enjoy it..You closed your eyes

Marilyn: Oh my god..Let me go Gary..I have work to do

Gary: Can we go out for dinner tonight to celebrate it

Marilyn: Celebrate what?..Our kiss

Gary: That too..To celebrate our husband and wife to be

Marilyn: Maybe..Let me find out how mom is doing..If she is ok..We can go out..If she is not too well..Sorry charming man

Gary: I understand..I respect that..I am mostly in love with your inner beauty..I like how much you care about your mom

Marilyn: Ok..Thank you..See you later

Gary: I will call you

Marilyn: No problem

Gary: No hug..No kiss?

Marilyn: You had enough kiss for the day sir

Gary: Where is the love?

Marilyn: Bye Gary..Don't beg

Gary: When it comes to your kiss I am not too proud to beg

Marilyn: Talk to you later

_Later that day

Marilyn: How was your day mom?

Mindy: Not too bad at all..When I got up to take my shower I was feeling some dizziness

Marilyn: You remember the doctor said that you might feel a little dizzy when you get up..Because you've been in bed for so long..The sudden change of position may cause dizziness

Mindy: I guess I stay in bed too long

Marilyn: You are fine mom..You need the rest..I don't want you to be in the kitchen cooking or cleaning the house

Mindy: I am not used to not doing anything..I don't know what to do with myself

Marilyn: You are ok..I am going to make dinner mom..What do you want?

Mindy: You don't have to make anything for me..I had some cereal not too long ago..I will be fine

Marilyn: Therefore..I am not cooking

Mindy: What are you going to eat?

Marilyn: I am invited out for dinner

Mindy: That's nice..Mark is trying to win your heart back

Marilyn: Mark cannot win my heart back..He stands a better chance of winning the lottery

Mindy: Really?..So..Who is the lucky guy?

Marilyn: You don't know him mom

Mindy: I know that..But..Does he have a name?

Marilyn: Mom..You are so nosy..What this information will do for you?

Mindy: You never know..His name might be a cure for cancer

Marilyn: Very funny mom..If you insist..Then I have to tell you..His name is Gary

Mindy: Gary..A nice name..This is such a coincidence..I knew a Gary when I was young

Marilyn: Here we go mom..He was a bad guy..Therefore this one is a bad guy too

Mindy: How do you know what I am going to say?

Marilyn: I know mom..I heard that story before..When I told you about Mark..You told me you knew a Mark..He was a bad guy..Blah..Blah..Blah

Mindy: Well..Where is Mark now?

Marilyn: I am no longer with him..But he was not a bad guy..Your prediction was not accurate..Now..Let's get straight to the point..How bad a person was the Gary that you knew?

Mindy: On the contrary..He was a very..Very nice man..He could have been your dad

Marilyn: My dad? How so?

Mindy: Well..We dated for a while..We were in love with each other and he moved away for college

Marilyn: You were cheating on dad..I thought you knew dad since high school

Mindy: Very funny..I was not cheating on your dad..I knew your dad since high school..But I was not dating your dad..Your dad and I started to date during my sophomore year in college

Marilyn: How did you meet with my dad?

Mindy: I knew your dad in high school..He was older than me..When I was in junior high he was in high school

Marilyn: How did you guys start the romance?

Mindy: How much time do you have?

Marilyn: I have some time

Mindy: Well..I was sitting on a bench outside the school library reading a book..When someone sat next to me

Colbert: Good morning..I said good morning

Mindy: Good morning..I am sorry I did not hear you

Colbert: I see..You were lost in you reading..It must be a very good book you are reading

Mindy: Well..I have to finish it soon because I have a paper to write about it

Colbert: You are not reading it because it is interesting..It is simply for academic purpose

Mindy: It's not a bad story but it would not have been my first choice..I am not an action freak

Colbert: You did not pick it..Did you?

Mindy: No I did not..The teacher required that I read it and write the paper

Colbert: By the way..My name is Colbert..And you are Mindy..Right?

Mindy: How do you know my name?

Colbert: You might not remember..But I was introduced to you once at Holly Name High

Mindy: Really?

Colbert: You don't remember that..Do you?

Mindy: I don't..I am sorry..I don't have a good memory

Colbert: I don't think I have such a good memory..It's just..I could not get your face and your name out of my mind

Mindy: I was that ugly back then

Colbert: That's the opposite..I thought you were very pretty

Mindy: I was pretty back then..Uh?..College can really makes one become ugly

Colbert: Sorry..I meant you were pretty back then and you are still gorgeous now

Mindy: What a smart guy..What is your major? Law?

Colbert: Why you asked?

Mindy: The ability with which you flip your tongue..Just like Michael Angelo flipped a brush to make what you said sound better

Colbert: It was not that hard at all..This is the truth..I haven't met another girl with that kind of beauty since

Mindy: Thank you..I am blushing

Colbert: I didn't mean to make you blush..By the way there is a party next Saturday..I would love to invite you to accompany me..Would you come?

Mindy: Maybe..If I received an invitation

Colbert: Very funny..I am inviting you now

Mindy: Well..You said..You would love to invite me..Would love..It was not definite

Colbert: Would you come with me

Mindy: I guess so..I am pretty boring..I don't drink alcohol and I am not much of a dancer

Colbert: Fine with me..My kind of guest

Mindy: Just curious..Your girlfriend is too tired to accompany you?

Colbert: My girlfriend will accompany me

Mindy: She will?

Colbert: Will you not?

Mindy: C'mon mister..Don't play with me..I was not born yesterday..You frat guys have the women at your feet..They are all players..Not that I am a selfish person but I am not too good at sharing a man

Colbert: Really?

Mindy: Before you go any further..It is not because a man is so important to me..It is simply that I don't want to be involved in promiscuity

Colbert: I am not one of those guys who practice promiscuity..I am a one woman at time guy..When I love a woman..I love her whole

Mindy: What do you mean you love her whole?

Colbert: Meaning there is no room for distraction..This is why I am very picky in term of what kind of woman I fall in love with..I know no one is perfect..But..She needs to have many aspects that I love so I don't have to look for an aspect in another woman

Mindy: What aspects are those?

Colbert: She needs to be a beautiful woman

Mindy: What do you mean by beautiful woman?

Colbert: She needs to be beautiful inside and out..More so the inside beauty

Mindy: You don't want a bitch uh?

Colbert: No man does..Most men are looking for peace of mind..When he gets home..Give him his food..Remote control..News paper..Life is beautiful

Mindy: Really? Men are that simple?

Colbert: Very simple..The women that figured that out..Stay married for long time..Those who think being married is an opportunity to harass the man..Thinking he is mine..Next thing you know..The man is looking for good time..Peaceful time somewhere else

Mindy: That's all it takes..Uh?

Colbert: One more important aspect is the sex..If you don't it..The man will go get it somewhere else

Mindy: I think you should teach a class on relationship

Colbert: Those are things I learned from my grandma

Mindy: Really?..Lucky you..You had a grandma to talk to you about those things

Colbert: Well..But your mom talked to you about men

Mindy: Never..My mom would never have such conversation with me..My parents were very conservative..Old school

Colbert: Maybe..Because I am man..She was feeling more comfortable to talk to me about women

Mindy: Boys got away with murder but the girls could not like a fly

Colbert: I know..So we are going to the party?

Mindy: I guess..Too bad I am not going to write the paper

Colbert: Why not?

Mindy: Well..If only I had the chance to finish reading my book

Colbert: I am sorry..I am leaving..But before I go..Can we go to the movie today?

Mindy: I am not much of a going out person..I am a nerdy girl

Colbert: Nerdy girl is a good thing..Let's go to the movie today

Mindy: Not today..I have class early..At seven in the morning..I have to be in bed early..Maybe Friday

Colbert: Ok..Friday we will g to the movie..I am looking forward to that

Mindy: See you Friday

Colbert: Ok..I am going to eat or sleep until Friday

Mindy: So..That's the way our romance started

Marilyn: Wow..Dad was a pretty smooth guy

Mindy: Of course..He was a gentleman..After I started to date him..My college years became fun..He introduced me to his friends..I became friends with the girls associated with the frat..It was fun a fun time

Marilyn: When did you introduce him to grandpa?

Mindy: Did I ever..I introduced him to my mom..My dad did not have time for that..He did not want to hear about boys talking to his daughters..I don't remember introduced him to my dad at all..I think my mom did introduce them..He proposed to me that same week

Marilyn: Oh my god..Dad was scared

Mindy: He would not say he was scared..But he knew how my dad was feeling about the situation..So he wanted to ease out the tension..So he did the right thing..He proposed to me..Well..Not before he asked my dad for my hand

Marilyn: My dad had been through a lot with your family

Mindy: Not really..That was the norm back then

Marilyn: Very nice story mom..I have to get ready..Gary will be here to pick me up..I have to hurry

Mindy: No..Don't hurry..You have to make him wait a little..That's the way it was done before..The woman makes the man wait when he arrives for a date

Marilyn: Why?..That's silly

Mindy: It was not silly..She did that to show the man that she is not easy..And not too excited about running out with him

Marilyn: Mom..If you were dating these days..You will have no play at all..No man has time for that anymore..You are late..He goes to the next girl

Mindy: That's the way it is now

Marilyn: Not like that..But..If a girl plays too conservative..Make him wait..Shows lack of interest..Most likely he will move on

Mindy: Well..This is a test..That's the way you see how committed he is

Marilyn: Mom..This is two thousand sixteen..By the time you are done seeing how committed he is..Another girl is done seeing how good he is in bed

Mindy: Really?

Marilyn: It is dogs eat dogs out there mom..Nobody has time for shy girls anymore..Bad girls get all the men

Mindy: Really?

Marilyn: I am only kidding mom..Bad girls don't get all the good men..I have to take my shower mom..It's getting late

Mindy: Go ahead

_ A month later at the work place

Gary: What's wrong? You have not been yourself the last couple days..What's wrong?

Marilyn: Something really bad happened to me last week

Gary: What is it babe?

Marilyn: I did not want to tell you..I did not want you to worry

Gary: Are you pregnant?

Marilyn: No..I used protection every time..No..Not that

Gary: What is it then?

Marilyn: I got stuck by a dirty syringe last week

Gary: Really?..You will be fine babe..That's why you are worried?

Marilyn: I found out that the patient is HIV positive

Gary: Really?..Maybe it is in your mind..It probably did not puncture the glove

Marilyn: Gary..C'mon..It did..I was bleeding

Gary: did you double glove

Marilyn: No I did not..I don't feel comfortable using double gloves

Gary: Did you tell Mrs. Franklin about it?

Marilyn: You are the first I told since that happened

Gary: You should tell her

Marilyn: You know what she said about double gloves..If you don't wear double gloves and something happens you will be fired..That's what she said

Gary: What do you want to do?

Marilyn: What do you mean?

Gary: You can't be worried about that all your life..You should get tested..And find out whether you are infected or not

Marilyn: Oh my god..I have so much to deal with..Now this..Why me? I am really tired of all these bad things that are happening in my life..Lost my dad..Mom has cancer and now this..What if I am tested positive?

Gary: There is no what if Marilyn..You will cross the bridge when you get there

Marilyn: Why me?

Marilyn: This is life..There will be obstacles in your way every day..You can't give up..You have to keep going through the obstacles..I am with you

Marilyn: Gary..What is "you are with me" can do in this situation?..Nothing..If I am positive..Who's going to take care of my mom?

Gary: Marilyn..You need to get tested

Marilyn: Why? I remember when my dad found out that he had cancer..His health got deteriorated quickly..I don't want the same thing to happen to me

Gary: You health will deteriorated anyway if you are to live your life worrying about it..The sooner you find out about your status the better

Marilyn: The sooner..The better..There is no cure for the disease

Gary: I know..But there are treatments

Marilyn: What treatment Gary? Those pills cost five hundred dollars..I am per-diem here with no health insurance..I can't afford the treatments that are available

Gary: Listen..Don't push the worry too far before finding out about your status..You are maybe fine..You are fine..You are just worrying for no reason..Let's get something to eat..And let me see that beautiful smile of yours

Marilyn: I am not in the mood to smile or eat Gary

Gary: So what you are going to do Marilyn..Lie down and die?..I suggest you get tested tomorrow

Marilyn: Where?..I don't have money for any expensive test right now..I have to pay my rent this week

Gary: The testing is free..There are many clinics that offer free testing..I will take tomorrow off to go with you

Marilyn: You don't have to..I can go by myself

Gary: I want to go with you..Just for support babe..No matter the result I will be by your side

Marilyn: This is what you are saying now..If I am found positive..You will disappear

Gary: I am not that kind of person..I am not the kind that turns my back on people when things get tough..Most people will talk to you..Will be your friend when things are lovely..But when you are in a difficult situation you become invisible..I am not that kind of a human being..This is a promise I made to you..So..Tomorrow we will go

_The next morning..Marilyn called her job to tell them that she will take half a day off

Mrs. Franklin: Hello

Marilyn: Hello..Mrs. Franklin..Good morning

Mrs. Franklin: Good morning Marilyn..Are you ok? You don't sound too good

Marilyn: I am ok..I have a little inconvenience..I will arrive at work a little late today

Mrs. Franklin: No problem..Fine..I will tell Suzanne to cover for you..See you later

Marilyn: I am sorry about the inconvenience

Mrs. Franklin: Don't you worry..Take care..I will see you later..Gary called out also..But..Today is not a busy day..It should not be a problem

Marilyn: Thank you

Mrs. Franklin: You are welcome

Mindy: Marilyn..I heard a car in the driveway

Marilyn: This is Gary..He is here to pick me up

Mindy: Where are you guys going..What's wrong with your car?

Marilyn: Mom..Mind your business please

Mindy: It is my business

Marilyn: Your business is to take your medicine and get stronger..That's all

Mindy: Why you sound so mean today?

Marilyn: I am not mean mom..I am just saying..Stop being nosy

Mindy: Whatever..Have a good day

Gary: Good morning..I said good morning

Marilyn: I heard you Gary..Good morning..My mind was a little far..I had a fight with my mom

Gary: Why fighting?

Marilyn: Not a fight per say..She was being nosy..She wanted to know why you are here to pick me up..Where I was going

Gary: Those are just normal questions..You got upset because of your state of mind..Remember..No matter what you are going through..Someone else is in a worse situation..You can't make anyone pay or be responsible..Be graceful to everyone..They did not cause you to be in that situation..This is a sign of courage when you carry your burden and don't try to make others pay by getting upset at them..If someone knows your situation and is trying to make it worse..Sticking a knife in the wound..It's a different story..Let them have it..But..Otherwise just be kind and courageous..No matter the result you will need a great attitude to fight that battle..One thing for sure..I Am With You..You hear me?

Marilyn: I hear you Gary..And I appreciate your support..I just cannot talk much..My mind is racing..I am very afraid..What will happen to my mom?..What will happen to me? If I am positive

Gary: You will cross the bridge when you get there..Worry does not solve problems..It only makes it worse..This is the place..Right?

Marilyn: Yes..What do I tell the people?

Gary: Nothing..Just tell them you are here to have an HIV test

Marilyn: I don't want them to think that I am a drug user or a promiscuous person

Gary: It does not matter what people think or say..People are going to say whatever they want anyway..Don't worry so much about what you can't change..Some people will go out of their way to try to make your life more difficult..Because a lot of people feel good when someone else is feeling bad..Some of them don't feel so good about themselves..So they are trying to be mean to someone else..A lot of people who are overweight behave that way..Don't be surprised if you see someone on a wheelchair trying to do something to make some else feel bad..Because hurt people hurt people..The people who mostly do things to hurt others are the ones who don't feel good about themselves..They just want to steal your joy..You have to get a thick skin..Because if you are sick..Not everybody will be kind to you

Marilyn: I hear you Gary..I am going in..You want to come with me?

Gary: Sure..Why not?..Let me park the car properly

_Inside the clinic

Marilyn: Good morning

Nurse: Good morning..How can I help you?

Marilyn: I am here to get an HIV test

Nurse: Ok..How long have you been a drug addict?

Marilyn: I am not a drug addict

Nurse: You are one of those happy girls?

Marilyn: I don't know what you mean?

Nurse: You know what I mean..Promiscuous woman

Marilyn: I am neither

Nurse: I was not born yesterday..You are in denial like all of them

Gary: Ma'am..I think you are being very unprofessional to talk to her this way

Nurse: Who are you her pimp?

Gary: Marilyn..Where are you going?

Marilyn: I am leaving..I can't take that kind of abuse

Gary: listen to me..This is exactly what I was trying to tell you..You have to build a tough skin

Marilyn: She is just being mean and disrespectful for no reason at all

Gary: remember..She is probably unhappy..Her life is miserable..She just wants to share the misery with you..Remember Marilyn..Hurt people..Hurt people

Marilyn: What do you mean?

Gary: Some people when they are hurting..Experiencing some type of discomfort..They have a tendency of being mean to others

Marilyn: I don't know her..She does not know me

Gary: It does not matter..She does not have to know you..All she has to know it's something to do that will cause you some discomfort..Or hurt you..Some people don't like to build their buildings to reach the height of yours..They prefer to tear yours down to the height of theirs..So..Now..I want you to go back in there and do what you came here to do..Ignore her..Just say to yourself..She hates on me because she is unhappy..Happy people don't have time for pettiness..Let's go

Nurse: Oh..You decided to come back?

Gary: Yes..She did..You want to know why?

Nurse: Why? Mr. Pimp

Gary: Well..I am not a pimp..This is only a product of your mind..Confectioned in your inner self..It only reflects what is running through your veins

Nurse: Whatever is running through my veins..I am not the one who needs an HIV test

Gary: You are so unprofessional

Nurse: Unprofessional or not..You and your queen there cannot and will never be able to do what I do..What do you do besides being a pimp?

Gary: Well I am only a medical student..I will be a doctor in four more years..And I wish not to work with anyone with your attitude and tone

Nurse: I am really sorry..I did not know you were a medical student..I apologize

Gary: Well..There is no need to apologize to me..Apologize to her..For assuming that she was a prostitute..For saying that I was her pimp..She is decent young lady..She is not at all promiscuous as you implied..She is just a young woman who has recently lost her dad to cancer..Her mother is now fighting for her life with the same disease..You have to be kind to everyone you meet because you never know what battle he or she is fighting..Right now she is dealing with all that she can handle..On top of it she was stuck with a dirty needle at her job..She is far from being all those adjectives that you have attributed to her

Nurse: I am so sorry young lady..You are making me cry

Gary: I don't mean to make you cry..Just be a little kinder to those you encounter..Address others with a kinder tone..It does not matter what you are dealing with in your personal life..It is a sign of courage to treat others with respect and kindness no matter what you are going through..Tone is a very important thing..The tone makes a song..Have you heard that before?

Nurse: No

Gary: Well..Let me explain..Some song will make you cry regardless that you understand the language or not..The tone will touch your heart..The melody..This is how important tone is..This not for no reason people have a tendency to talk to small baby a certain way..The way you say good morning to somebody can really help that person

Nurse: I am really sorry..Do you accept my apology young lady?

Gary: Her name is Marilyn

Nurse: Do you accept my apology Marilyn?

Marilyn: I am fine..No problem..What do I do next..I have to return to work when I leave here

Nurse: You are done with the application?

Marilyn: Yes I am done..Right here it says that it is optional to write your name on the application

Nurse: Yes..You may choose to do the test anonymously

Marilyn: I see

Nurse: I will take the application..Just go to that room aver there and that nurse will do the test for you

Marilyn: Am I going to endure the same amount of abuse again?

Nurse: No..You will be fine..I am so sorry

Marilyn: I am fine..I was just messing with you

Nurse: I learned so much today

Marilyn: Every day is a chance to learn..Life is classroom

_Marilyn is done with the test and headed to work..Later that day on her way home..While in the car with Gary she received a call..Let's listen:

Gary: Your phone babe

Marilyn: I am not in the mood to talk to anyone now

Gary: Answer it..It could be your mom

Marilyn: Hello

Nurse: Hello..Is this Marilyn?

Marilyn: Yes..This is she

Nurse: I am a nurse from the medical center..You took an HIV test this morning..Right?

Marilyn: Yes I did..Is there a problem

Nurse: No..There is no problem

Marilyn: Am I tested positive? You can tell me

Nurse: I don't know the result of your test ma'am..The director asked me to call you

Marilyn: To call me for what?

Nurse: He wants to discuss the result of the test with you

Marilyn: So..It is positive..Right?

Nurse: Dr Harper did not say..He simply said it is regarding the result

Marilyn: Oh god..Oh god..I am positive

Nurse: Well..Don't jump to conclusion too quickly..There are sometimes some false positives..You may have to take the test again..If in fact it is positive..But..We don't know yet..When can you come for a face to face with doctor Harper?

Marilyn: Oh my god..Oh god..Help me

Nurse: You will be fine

Marilyn: Tomorrow..Tell him tomorrow

Nurse: At what time?

Marilyn: It does not matter..I am going to die anyway

Nurse: No..Don't talk that way..People live long as long you take the medications..You will be alright

Marilyn: Medications..I can't afford any of that

Nurse: I will tell Harper that you will be in to see him in the morning

Marilyn: Tell him ten o'clock

Nurse: Thank you..You have a good day

Gary: What did she say, babe?..The test is positive?

Marilyn: She did not say that..But..The way she is talking..I know it is..The director of the center..Dr. Harper wants to see me

Gary: Really?

Marilyn: Yes Gary..I might be positive..Are you ready to run now?

Gary: Don't talk to me this way..I told you already..I am not that kind of person..Running where?..We are all human..And diseases don't fall on trees..You have to believe me..I am with you

Marilyn: Tomorrow..I have to meet with that doctor

Gary: We are not going to speculate or jump to conclusion..Let's wait and see what he wants to talk about

Marilyn: Gary..What do you think he wants to talk to me about..The weather?

Gary: Let's wait and see..I will come with you tomorrow

Marilyn: No you don't have to..You have already taken too many days off..You will get fired

Gary: I don't care about that..I just want to be there for you..Are you going to tell your mom about it?

Marilyn: No..Not at all..Mom is the last person to tell something like that to..She would die

Gary: Tomorrow I will pick you up..You want to go get something to eat?

Marilyn: No..I am not hungry..I don't feel like eating anything

Gary: What have you eaten since morning? Nothing..Let's go..You will take it home with you

Marilyn: You just don't understand Gary..You don't understand the situation that I am in right now

Gary: I understand babe..You don't need to cry..Everything is going to be fine

Marilyn: You are just saying that to make me feel good..How everything is going to be fine

Gary: You remember..Magic Johnson was HIV positive..He is still alive..Enjoying his life

Marilyn: Gary..I am not Magic Johnson..Magic is a super star..He has a lot of money..He could afford everything that is out there that would keep him alive and well

Gary: I know..But He had a positive attitude as well..That counts a lot

Marilyn: The virus does not care whether you have a positive attitude or not..You will just die with a positive attitude..Why me?..That day I wanted to stay home..I did not feel well at all..I should have stayed home

Gary: Babe..You can live in the past..I should.."I should" will not return the time..That's the past..There is an author called Phito Polycarpe..He said:

"To be living in the past

It is simply allowing your pain to last

Embrace this new day and have a blast"

Marilyn: That's a very beautiful quote..But what new day Gary?..I am going to die soon

Gary: You are not..You have to be ready to fight..And what are we talking about anyway? Who said that you are HIV positive?

Marilyn: Gary..You have to be realistic..This is hanging on to false hope..The doctor wants to talk to me..Why would that man want to talk to me?

Gary: You never know..We are here at the place..What do you want me to order you?

Marilyn: I could not tell you..I have no need for food right now

Gary: I will get you something anyway

Marilyn: Gary..Don't take too long in there..I am not feeling good..I want to go home and lay down

Gary: I will be back in a minute

Marilyn: You are back already?

Gary: I told you..That's what I like about this place..They don't waste time at all

Marilyn: Gary..Where are you going..You are passing my house

Gary: Sorry..I did not realize that we were here already..Why there is no light..Mo is not there?

Marilyn: She is there..She just likes to keep the house dark..She is probably sleeping

Gary: Babe..Take your food

Marilyn: Thank you..Call me when you get home

Gary: Ok..Talk to you soon..Bye

Marilyn: Bye..Your phone is ringing

Gary: Later babe..Hello

Thomas: Gary..What's going on buddy?

Gary: I did not hear from you yesterday

Thomas: All the guys were at my house..We watched the game here

Gary: I could not come..I was not in the mood

Thomas: What's wrong with you..You are probably too in love with your girl..What's her name..Marilyn

Gary: Well..There are some issues there..My mind is not quite at peace

Thomas: Romantic problem already?..That early?

Gary: No man..It is more than that

Thomas: She is pregnant?

Gary: No..Not that..Why don't you stop by..I will talk to you about it

Thomas: What is it that you can't discuss over the phone..Is she a man?

Gary: Very funny Thomas..C'mon..Don't be ridiculous

Thomas: Well these days..A transgender looks just like a woman

Gary: I don't get fool that easy

Thomas: This is why I check to see if there is a package at first meeting

Gary: Thomas..I am not in a mood to joke now

Thomas: It must be serious then

Gary: Stop by dude..I have some food

Thomas: Should I bring some beers?

Gary: Thomas..This a week day

Thomas: Just a couple

Gary: I guess..I am stressed anyway

Thomas: See you soon brother

_Meanwhile at Marilyn's home

Mindy: I cook you something

Marilyn: I am not in a mood to eat

Mindy: What is wrong baby?..You are not the Marilyn that I know..Tell mommy what is wrong

Marilyn: Everything is ok mom

Mindy: Is it me you are worrying about?

Marilyn: Mom..I should not?..Of course I am mom

Mindy: You should not worry so much about me..The last couple days you seem very depressed

Marilyn: I am fine mom

Mindy: Your phone is ringing

Marilyn: Hello

Gary: Hello babe

Marilyn: Yes..Are you home?

Gary: Yes..I just got home..Thomas is on his way here

Marilyn: Ok..I am going to bed and rest

Gary: No problem..Call me whenever you please..How is your mom doing?

Marilyn: Mom is ok..She is just being annoying

Gary: What did she do?

Marilyn: You know mom..The usual..Being nosy..She said I look depressed

Gary: Well..She is probably right..You have to change your attitude..Have a more positive attitude..Don't be so gloomy..You have to get ready to fight for your life..You don't even have the result yet and you look defeated..You can't be like that

Marilyn: I understand..I want to keep the result a secret from my mom..I just don't have to lie to her every time I have to go to the doctor

Gary: You know..Keeping a secret for someone who should I have known about something is worse than lying..It is more deceitful than lying..For instance..I you know something is happening to someone and you participate in holding it as a secret..You are more than a liar..You are in fact a conspirator..This is how a conspiracy is created..Conspiracy is based on secret..Secret for one good reason to create and fabricate defamation..The key to keeping the defamation a secret is simply so the victim does not know what is going on and challenge it..People have a tendency to that..To be part of a large group..This is how bullying operates..Someone is being bullied and everybody joined the bully..It is nothing new

Marilyn: I understand..You right about that..When I was in high school..There was a guy called David..He was being bullied..They always found something wrong about him..No matter how well he did..They tried to find a reason to try to humiliate him..The bully side is a good side for those who have chips on their shoulders..For those who enjoy throwing stones and hide their hands..For those who are insecure about themselves..For those who are jealous

Gary: Exactly..I am not good at keeping secret..Especially if it is related to injustice..Whenever you see one person is the topic of everyone..Beware..Something fishy is going on..He or she might be so good they can't afford not to talk about

Marilyn: The people who are more active in doing so are usually the wish list people..Those who wished they could do what that person is capable of doing

Gary: You are so right

Marilyn: I used to tell David to ignore them...And he did..It was a campaign of make believe that David was a bad person..He did not give a damn about them..The funny thing was..He did not even see them and they were constantly talking about him

Gary: That explains it all..He was important enough to get a lot of attention from them while he did not even know they exist..When that happens..Simply let it be..Because empty cans make more noise..They are going to try every trick to create distraction..Just remain focused..The dogs bark but you keep on walking

Marilyn: Ok..I am going to bed Gary

Gary: Talk to you tomorrow..Ok babe..Thomas is here

Marilyn: Good bye

_Meanwhile at Gary's apartment

Gary: You are here already Tom?

Thomas: Yeah man..I only live a few miles away

Gary: I know..This is why I am asking you how you get here in two minutes

Thomas: You right about that..I just wanted to try the new turbo I put on the mustang

Gary: Tom..Vehicles are not to be played with..They can be as dangerous as a weapon

Thomas: I know..I know..I am not here to hear you preach..I am here for two reasons

Gary: What are those two reasons brother?

Thomas: The food and the beers..Well..One more reason

Gary: What is it?

Thomas: You said you needed to talk to me about something serious

Gary: That should have been the main reason

Thomas: Before the beer and the food? You are insane..What is it you wanted to talk about?

Gary: Let's get the food and beers and go on the porch

Thomas: Gary..Where are the forks?

Gary: There are some plastic ones in the bag

Thomas: You know I don't use plastic forks..Where are the real forks?

Gary: Tom..How long you've been coming here? You know where I keep the forks

Thomas: I could not find any where they used to be

Gary: Look in the drawer near the refrigerator

Thomas: Why you put them there?

Gary: I did not do it..Marilyn did that

Thomas: She rearranged everything..This is why your apartment looks so well put together..How is she doing?

Gary: She is ok..This is why I wanted to talk to you

Thomas: What happens?..There is trouble in paradise already?

Gary: Well..Everything is fine between us

Thomas: What is it then that you want to talk about?

Gary: Well..She took the HIV test this week

Thomas: Why she took the HIV test?..She does drugs?

Gary: No..She does not

Thomas: She used to be promiscuous?

Gary: No..Not at all

Thomas: So..Why she needed the test for?

Gary: Well..She was stuck by a hypodermic needle at her job

Thomas: What is a hypodermic needle?

Gary: That is the needle that is attached to a syringe

Thomas: Ok..So it was a dirty?

Gary: Yes..She used on a patient and the patient was HIV positive

Thomas: Really? That's really scary..What are you going to do..You are going to leave her..Right?

Gary: Of course not..Why should I?

Thomas: Are you nuts?

Gary: What do you mean?

Thomas: I think it would be stupid to be with a woman that has AIDS

Gary: First of all Thomas..HIV is not AIDS

Thomas: It is the same thing

Gary: No..They are not..You need to educate yourself

Thomas: Tell me about..All I need to know is somebody has HIV or AIDS so I can stay away from them

Gary: Thomas..Don't talk so ignorantly..I am disappointed in you

Thomas: You can be as disappointed as you can be..Guess what?..I will be alive

Gary: People are so ignorant about that illness..I am not saying one should not be careful or cautious..I am a medical student Gary..I know what I am talking about

Thomas: I remember last year there was a guy in school who had HIV..He wanted to shake my hand..I did not

Gary: That was wrong Thomas..You can't catch the disease by shaking someone's hand..You can only get the disease by exchange of body fluids..If you had a cut in your hand and he happed to have an open wound or blood on his hand that could have put you at risk

Thomas: I just did not want to get the HIV and AIDS

Gary: They are two different things..When you are HIV positive the virus was detected in your blood..In your system..AIDS is simply when your immune system is overwhelmed and destroyed by the virus

Thomas: I see..So she is positive?

Gary: Don't know yet..Tomorrow she will find out

Thomas: So..What are you going to do Gary..You can't be with someone who is HIV positive

Gary: What do you mean?

Thomas: You just can't be with somebody that can contaminate you and kill you

Gary: Thomas..I was with her before that..We are jumping to conclusion here..We don't yet whether she is positive or not..Either way my brother..I can't turn my back on her just because she is sick..If everybody turns their backs on those who are sick what would happen to those sick people

Thomas: Gary..I am in your best interest..You are like a brother to me..You have your whole life to live..You are working on becoming a doctor..Why would jeopardize all that by staying with a woman who has a contagious disease?

Gary: You want to know why?

Thomas: Yes..Tell me why?

Gary: The same reason you would like me to still be your friend if you were the one infected with a contagious disease

Thomas: Well..If I was infected with a contagious disease..You would not have to hold my hand..Hug me..Sleep near me..You are in a relationship with that girl..How will you keep the relationship alive?

Gary: The same way I keep my friendship alive

Thomas: Gary..Don't be ridiculous..We are buddies..You don't have buddy contact..She is your girlfriend..Don't you think it's time to get away..Or soon you will be infected too

Gary: Thomas my friend..I don't want you to take what I am going to say the wrong way

Thomas: What is it you are going to say?

Gary: You might be HIV positive now

Thomas: Who are you talking about? Me?

Gary: Yes..You

Thomas: That's ridiculous..You are not making any sense

Gary: Yes I am..How many women you have been with on campus..Just on campus..Since you started school?

Thomas: Why?

Gary: Answer me..Be as honest as possible

Thomas: How am I going to answer that question..You know I don't kiss and tell

Gary: You don't have to say names..How many brothers?

Thomas: I would say twenty

Gary: Thomas..C'mon? Twenty?..You mean the first year?

Thomas: I can't be accurate..I don't keep count

Gary: You remember last semester..You were trying to have sex with as many freshmen as you can

Thomas: Be careful now..Not freshmen..Freshwomen

Gary: You know what I mean..You had sex with at least forty different girls that semester

Thomas: You are right

Gary: Thank you..I know I am right..Do you really believe all those women that you had sex with are all HIV negative?

Thomas: I think so

Gary: You think so..But you are not sure..How many times did you use a condom during sex?

Thomas: None..I can't tolerate condoms..Some of the girls are allergic to condoms

Gary: Chance is..One of those women that you had sex with might be HIV positive my friend

Thomas: This is scary

Gary: You might be positive now..But I am still your friend..Am I not?

Thomas: Well

Gary: Am I not your friend..You just used my fork to eat..Did you not?

Thomas: What are you trying to say..You don't want me to use stuff from your apartment

Gary: This is not what I am trying to say my brother..I just want you to realize that you don't have to treat someone who is tested positive so differently..I am trying to educate you

Thomas: I see your point

Gary: If I were you I would go get a test done

Thomas: Man please..I am fine..You are crazy..Why you think I should do so?

Gary: With all the booty you've been getting on campus..I think you should

Thomas: I will do that when I start coughing

Gary: Really?

Thomas: Yes..When I have a cold or a cough that I can't shake off it will be time to test

Gary: Very funny..Then it will be too late..That means you already has AIDS

Thomas: Once you get it it's too late anyway..Isn't it?

Gary: Thomas..I am done arguing with you..One thing I want to ask you..If she is positive..If don't feel comfortable being around her..It's fine..But..I don't want you to come around and act ignorant and hurt her feelings

Thomas: I am good man..I understand you..You made a good point by telling me that I deal with people every day and I don't even know whether they are positive or not

Gary: I am glad that you understand brother..Now it's time to get going

Thomas: You are putting me out

Gary: Thomas..This is a week day..This weekend I might hang out with you guys

Thomas: What do you mean by might?

Gary: It all depends on the result of her test..If she is positive..I have to be with her and give her all the support she needs

Thomas: I respect that

Gary: Good..It means a lot to me coming from you

Thomas: Really?..You think I am a heartless person Gary?

Gary: Not really..I just think you need to use your heart more often

Thomas: I use it every second..It's beating in my chest

Gary: Why don't you use to beat yourself out of my place?

Thomas: Very funny Gary..You invited me over..Now you put me out..What kind of friend are you?

Gary: The kind who knows how to put a friend out on a week day

Thomas: You have class tomorrow..I will see you on campus

Gary: Maybe not

Thomas: You are working at that place?

Gary: I will go to the place with her to get the result..Then I will stay with her the rest of the day..I don't have classes tomorrow

Thomas: See you buddy..Thanks for the food

Gary: You are welcome..Thanks for stopping by

Thomas: Even though you put me out

Gary: Take the rest of the food with you Tom

Thomas: I am good thanks..I wish her luck

Gary: Well..It is probably too late for luck..It's either she is positive or not

Thomas: It's terrible

Gary: I know..But she is a fighter..She will put a good fight..Later buddy

Thomas: Alright my dude..Peace

_The next morning

Mindy: Marilyn..You are up so early..What time is it?..It's only three in the morning

Marilyn: I needed to go to bathroom mom

Mindy: You did not sleep at all last night..I heard you walking..Then I heard your TV on all night

Marilyn: I just could not sleep mom

Mindy: Your eyes look so red..Were you crying?

Marilyn: I am fine mom

Mindy: I gave birth to you..I know you better than you think..Something is wrong..Are you going to tell me?

Marilyn: Mom..Don't worry about me so much..You have to gather your strength to beat the cancer..This is no time to be worried about me

Mindy: What is it about..Are you having problem with Gary?

Marilyn: No mom..Gary is fine..He has been very nice to me

Mindy: Is it because you stopped going to school?

Marilyn: No mom..Let me go back to bed..I can't talk much..You are questioning me to death

Mindy: You are my daughter..We live together..If something is wrong you have to tell me

Marilyn: Mom..Go back to bed

_Five hours later

Mindy: Gary is here Marilyn

Marilyn: Tell him to wait for me a minute..I will be ready soon

Mindy: Gary..Have a seat..She is putting on her makeup..She will be ready in a minute..Do you want a cup of coffee?

Gary: No thank you..I am not a coffee fanatic

Mindy: Well..I drink coffee all day..Five to six cups a day

Gary: My dad is the same way..He has to have his coffee wherever he goes

Mindy: Gary..Do you know what is wrong with my daughter? She has not been herself lately..I notice that her eyes were red..She has been crying

Gary: She is not very happy..But I could not tell you what is really wrong..Maybe she is concerned about you..She can wait for you to be cancer free

Mindy: She should not worry about me..I will be just fine..When you find out what is wrong with her..Let me know ok

Gary: I will

Mindy: She is ready..You see how beautiful my daughter is Gary

Gary: Yes..I certainly do..The apple did not fall far from the tree

Mindy: Well..Her father was a good looking man..Have you seen any picture of my husband?

Marilyn: Mom..We don't have time for that..We have to get going

Mindy: When you come by next time I will show you my album..My husband was very good looking..She gets my hair..But everything else is from her dad

Marilyn: Let's go Gary..If mom starts with dad stories we will never leave this place

Mindy: You have to come by to see me..Not to see Marilyn..But to see me so we can chat..And tell you about my husband

Gary: I will do that..You have a great day..I will see you later

Marilyn: See you later mom..Eat something..There is food in the in the fridge

Mindy: I will be fine baby..Have a great day guys

Marilyn: Why you park so far Gary?

Gary: It's not that far

Marilyn: It is so far we might as well call UBER to take us to the car

Gary: Very funny..This is the Marilyn I want to see..Be brave and ready to fight..Maintain your sense of humor

Marilyn: I am trying but sometimes I got overwhelmed by the thought of it..Not knowing what will happen..If I could afford the treatment..I would not have been so bad

Gary: We will find a way

Marilyn: Which way is that..You are going to steal medication from the pharmacy..You have insurance..Right?

Gary: Yes..My dad covers us all

Marilyn: Lucky you..When my dad was alive..I was under his policy..But my life has been sliding into a pitfall since he passed away..Things seem to be getting worse every day..Mom is sick..She has cancer..Now..I have an incurable disease

Gary: No you don't..Wait for the result

Marilyn: Gary please..Stop it..Why would those people want to see me for?

Gary: Wait.,Just wait

Marilyn: I will die anyway it's inevitable

Gary: Everybody will die anyway..You are not alone in this

Marilyn: I will die soon

Gary: No you will not..I will be there to help you fight

Marilyn: Ok..I heard that Gary..But..What are you?..Are you a medical cocktail against the disease?

Gary: I am not..But I am with you in this a thousand percent

Marilyn: Ok..I truly appreciate that..I really appreciate your kindness..But you don't have to put your life on hold for me..This is not your illness..Watch it Gary..Red light

Gary: I saw it babe

Marilyn: You are trying to kill me before the disease

Gary: What disease?

Marilyn: Whatever..We are almost here..You can stay in the car and I will go in there and talk to the doctor

Gary: No..I want to come in there with you

Marilyn: Why are you being so nosy Gary..This is not your business

Gary: It is my business

Marilyn: Since when that I was your business?

Gary: Since the very first time I saw you

Marilyn: Really?

Gary: Yes..Really

Marilyn: Take that spot babe

Gary: I was trying to find a closer one

Marilyn: Let's go

Gary: Are you ready?

Marilyn: Of course..I know what to expect already

Gary: Let's go..Watch your step..There is some water on the ground

Marilyn: I see it..Thanks..It rained so much last

Gary: I know..I left the window in the living room opened

Marilyn: Really?..Everything is wet?

Gary: No..Not really

Marilyn: Good morning

Nurse: Good morning..How can I help you?

Marilyn: I am here to see the director..I forgot his name

Nurse: Dr. Harper

Marilyn: Yes Dr. Harper..Is he here?

Nurse: Yes he is..But he is on the phone..I will let you know that you are here..Have a seat please

Gary: Do you have any magazines or the news paper here at all?

Nurse: Yes..They are right behind you

Gary: Thank you

Nurse: Let me let Dr. Harper know that you are here

Marilyn: Thanks

Nurse: Dr. Harper

Dr. Harper: Yes..Come in

Nurse: Doctor..Your nine o'clock is here

Dr. Harper: Ok..Pull out her file for me..Tell I will be out shortly

Nurse: Yes sir

Dr. Harper: Thank you..Hey Dora

Nurse: Yes

Dr. Harper: How many afternoon appointments do I have?

Nurse: You have just one

Dr. Harper: At what time?

Nurse: At two

Dr. Harper: Can you cancel it for me..Well..Just postpone it..Try to squeeze it into tomorrow schedule

Nurse: Yes..I can do that

Dr. Harper: It was not an urgent one..Was it?

Nurse: No it was not

Dr. Harper: Who is it?..Was it a new patient?

Nurse: No..Mr. Franklin

Dr. Harper: Ok

Nurse: If you want I can squeeze him in for later this afternoon

Dr. Harper: I don't think it's a good idea..I have a surgery at the hospital..I don't think I will done on time to come back to the office

Nurse: Ok..I will schedule it for tomorrow

Dr. Harper: Dora

Nurse: Yes

Dr. Harper: Did get the results from the lab yet?

Nurse: Not yet..They should arrive this afternoon

Dr. Harper: When they do let me know

Nurse: I will doctor..Should I bring the patient in now?

Dr. Harper: What patient?

Nurse: The young lady

Dr. Harper: She is not a patient..Is she your patient?

Nurse: No..I am sorry..I am so used to saying it..I am sorry..Should I bring her in?

Dr. Harper: Bring me her file first

Nurse: Ok..Coming up

Dr. Harper: Thank you

Nurse: Dr. Harper will see you soon

Marilyn: Thank you

Nurse: here is the file doctor Harper

Dr. Harper: Just bring her in please

Nurse: Yes sir

Gary: Did you see what happened last night?

Marilyn: You believe the things you see in the news paper?

Nurse: Miss..The doctor will see you now

Marilyn: Thank you

Gary: See you soon babe

Marilyn: Ok

Nurse: Here she is doctor

Dr. Harper: Good morning..Good morning

Marilyn: Good morning

Dr. Harper: Have a seat please

Marilyn: Thank you

Dr. Harper: Did it rain enough for you last night?

Marilyn: So much rain..I thought it was not going to stop

Dr. Harper: I live in this town for a long time..I have never seen so much rain

Marilyn: I was like a deluge

Dr. Harper: I live here maybe for longer than you have been on this planet..I've never see so much rain..How old are you?

Marilyn: I am twenty two

Dr. Harper: You are a baby..I live here in this town for thirty seven years

Marilyn: Wow..I was not born yet

Dr. Harper: Of course not..Your mom and dad did not probably meet each other yet?

Marilyn: You were born here?

Dr. Harper: No..I was born in the town next door..A tiny town called Sidney..Have you been there?

Marilyn: No..Not yet..I have heard of it..I heard it is one of the most beautiful towns in the state

Dr. Harper: Well..I will take the liberty to say in the whole country

Marilyn: Really? You are probably being bias

Dr. Harper: Not at all..You have to visit Sidney..I recommend it

Marilyn: Ok

Dr. Harper: How are you feeling today?

Marilyn: Very anxious..Scared to death

Dr. Harper: I understand..But..It is better to know your status than not to know..These days' people don't die of this disease as quick as they used to..And if you follow proper treatment you can live a regular long life

Marilyn: Do you have the result?

Dr. Harper: Yes I do

Marilyn: Is it positive?

Dr. Harper: It revealed that your body is creating anti body against the virus..This is what you called positive..Your body detected the virus and began to fight it

Marilyn: Oh god..What do I do?

Dr. Harper: There is nothing else to do but to fight..You don't drink alcohol..Right?

Marilyn: No I don't

Dr. Harper: You don't smoke..Right?

Marilyn: No..I don't smoke

Dr. Harper: You are a perfect candidate to put up a good fight against the disease..As long as you take your medication you will live

Marilyn: Oh god

Dr. Harper: No need to cry

Marilyn: I have been through so much within the last two years..I lost my dad to cancer..Now my mom is home sick..She too has cancer..And now I have this incurable disease

Dr. Harper: I know..It is in fact incurable..But it is manageable..The scientists are working every day feverishly to find a cure..Until that day comes..We have to fight with what we have..I will send you to a specialist..He is a good friend of mine..He will help you pick a great treatment plan in order to manage the disease..You don't have to cry..Do you have someone with you here?

Marilyn: Yes

Dr. Harper: Who is he?

Marilyn: His name is Gary

Dr. Harper: What is your relation with him?

Marilyn: He is my boyfriend

Dr. Harper: Do you want me to call him in?..Are you comfortable with that?

Marilyn: Yes..I have no problem with it

Dr. Harper: Hold on just a second

Marilyn: He is in the waiting area

Dr. Harper: Good morning

Gary: Good morning

Dr. Harper: Are you Gary

Gary: Yes sir..And you are?

Dr. Harper: Dr. Harper..Your fiancée is a very brave young lady..Do you mind join us?..I am discussing treatments and precaution with her..I think it would be great if I could talk to you as well..Do you mind?

Gary: No..Not at all..My pleasure

Dr. Harper: Come with me

Gary: Sure

Dr. Harper: I am back..And I bring with me someone you want to see..You were tired of seeing my face..Weren't you?

Marilyn: Not really

Gary: Hi babe

Marilyn: Hi

Dr. Harper: Have a seat please

Gary: Thank you

Dr. Harper: Gary..Congratulations..Your fiancée is not only beautiful but she is very intelligent and brave young lady

Gary: Thank you..I tell her that every day but she does not believe me

Dr. Harper: She is a good one..I know a good one when I see one..I am very experience in that matter..I am on my third marriage..It took me three marriages to get it right..But I get it

Gary: I hear you..Third time is always a charm..I hope to get it right the first time

Marilyn: You better

Dr. Harper: You have the right one

Gary: Thank you

Dr. Harper: Right before you came in..Marilyn and I were discussing treatments..As usual people get upset about learning their status..But it is not a death sentence..There are treatments out there that will keep you live a long normal life

Gary: I try to make her understand that

Marilyn: It is not I don't understand..But how am I going to pay for those medications

Dr. Harper: You don't have health coverage?

Marilyn: I don't..I had health coverage..But since my dad passed away..I haven't had any

Dr. Harper: Do you have health coverage Gary?

Gary: Yes I do..I am under my dad's policy

Dr. Harper: Where does he work?

Gary: He is a U.S. senator

Dr. Harper: I see..You have great coverage..What I can do for you Marilyn..I have a supply of samples right here..Those are cocktails use to contain the virus and boost your immune system..I will provide you with what I have here..It will probably last three months..During that time..You have to try your best to find a way to buy the medications..Otherwise it will be very difficult to fight the virus..I want to tell you what you should expect..You will experience cold sweat at night..You will lose weight..You will lose your hair..Not all your hair..But your hair will not be healthy..This is why you will need to take a lot of vitamin E..Try to take a lot of vitamin C as well..You don't want to catch a cold..Although it will be very easy to catch a cold as your immune system begins to deteriorated..And it will be harder to get rid of the cold..The virus does not kill you..It's the many illnesses..And viruses that attack the body that eventually kill the patient..Is there any way you could get her under your policy Gary?

Marilyn: No..His father covers him..No..There is no way..No..I will find a way

Gary: I could try to ask my dad

Marilyn: No Gary..Don't be ridiculous..Thanks anyway..But I will find a way

Dr. Harper: Here are the medications..It is called a cocktail because you need to take all of them together..If you miss one..It is as if you did not any at all..For it to be efficient you need to take all of them every day

Gary: It seems a lot of them

Dr. Harper: Yes..It's quite a bit..Twenty four pills

Gary: Every day?

Dr. Harper: Yes..Like I said..Until the scientists found a cure..This is what we must do to survive

Dr. Harper: I am going to write for you the order by which to take them

Marilyn: Thank you

Dr. Harper: One of them you need to take six pills..And the others are three each..Make sure you eat before taking the pills..If your stomach is kind of upset..Do not take them..Wait until you feel better..You don't need to vomit the pills..They are very expensive..Those did not cost you anything..But in the future when you started to buy them..You will realize how expensive they are..You can't afford to vomit or waste them

Gary: How soon she needs to start taking them

Dr. Harper: Like yesterday..Because the virus is already at work trying to destroy her immune system..You may feel light fever at night..This is your body fighting the virus..Actually the fever is a sign of being healthy..When the immune system is completely destroyed..There will be no more fever

Marilyn: How long do I have to live?

Dr. Harper: How long?..As long as anyone else..Then again..You need to take your medications..So keep me posted..And if you guys have any question..Feel free to contact me..Here's my card..Let me write my cell number on there for you

Marilyn: Thank you

Dr. Harper: And no more crying..This is the time to fight..This is nothing to be ashamed about..You were not using drugs..You were not promiscuous..You got infected at work..But..There such a stigma attached to the disease..Once you are positive..People insinuate that you were doing drugs or you were promiscuous..As long as your conscious is clean..You should not worry about what people think..Even if you were doing drugs or have been promiscuous..This is no time to be ashamed..Because you are fighting for your life..Do you guys have any question?

Gary: No..What about sex?..No sex at all?

Dr. Harper: Of course you can have sex..Remember..The disease can only be transmitted by exchange of body fluid..Use protection during sexual activities..Some women and men are allergic to latex..So..Find latex free protections

Gary: Thank you

Marilyn: Thank you

Dr. Harper: You are very welcome..Did I answer all your questions?

Gary: I think so..Do you have any question babe?

Marilyn: No..I am fine

Dr. Harper: Try not to run out of medication..Try your best to get some type of coverage..Although it's going to be difficult to coverage after you've been tested positive..But..Try your very best to get the medications..That's your only chance to survive

Marilyn: Ok..Thank you Dr. Harper

Dr. Harper: Remember..Stay in touch..Let me know how you are doing

_On the way home

Marilyn: What am I going to do Gary?..Oh my god..My mom's cancer was all I could bare..Now this..God..Why me? ..I was always careful..I was never promiscuous..I did not do drugs..But yet..I am infected with that disease

Gary: Don't you worry about it..God has a plan for you..Maybe out of this will come something great

Marilyn: What great thing could come out of this?..My death..That's the only great thing that could come out of this situation

Gary: God always has a mysterious way of doing thing..Let's not be pessimistic

Marilyn: Pessimistic?..Gary..I am dying..What do you want to be..Optimistic about dying a slow death

Gary: Remember what the doctor said..You will not die as long as you take your medication

Marilyn: I only have medication for only three months..After those three months Gary what am I going to do?

Gary: We will find a way..I will talk to my dad and see if he will put you under his health plan

Marilyn: Gary..Please..Don't even talk this way to me..Why would you ask your dad to put me under his plan..I am not his daughter..Don't be ridiculous

Gary: Why not?

Marilyn: This is absurd..Not only that..It is too late for me to get coverage right now..I am already positive..I f the insurance is charged for HIV medications..Don't you think they will investigate to find out when I was tested positive..In the application you have to fill out..They ask for status

Gary: I understand..We will find a way

Marilyn: Gary..I think you are in denial

Gary: Denial of what?

Marilyn: In denial that I will soon die

Gary: Of course I am in denial because you will not die soon

Marilyn: I don't feel like going to work..I don't feel good at all

Gary: Well..Call and let them know that you can't come..I am not going either..I will stay with you

Marilyn: I don't want them to be short of staff

Gary: Today is Tuesday..They have a full crew..They should be alright

Marilyn: What do I tell my mom?..Oh my god..What am I going to do?..My stomach is hurting me..I am feeling sick already

Gary: Babe it's in your mind..You need to understand..That is devastating news..So..Your body and your psyche are trying to cope with it..After a while you will learn to live with it..My phone is ringing

Marilyn: It's right here

Gary: Thanks..Hello

Thomas: Hey Gary..How are you buddy

Gary: I am good..I am driving Marilyn home

Thomas: Ok..She is not dead yet?

Gary: Thomas..This is not funny..Be more responsible..You are not a child..This is nothing to be playing with

Thomas: I am sorry..I was just joking..C'mon Gary..You know me better than that

Gary: I don't know you right now..

Thomas: C'mon

Gary: Good bye..I have to go

Thomas: Listen Ga..

Marilyn: What happened?..You hung up on him?

Gary: Yeah

Marilyn: Why..He is one of your best friends..Don't be like that..You were telling me not to be moody and be nice to others..Don't let the situation dictate how I treat people..Now..You are doing the same thing

Gary: No..That's something else

Marilyn: Call him back Gary

Gary: Marilyn..Stop..He deserves it

Marilyn: What did he say to you..He is your friend

Gary: He said something that I did not like

Marilyn: I don't think you are setting a good example..I need somebody next to me that will be strong and not snap on his friends and everybody else

Gary: I told you that he said something I did not like

Marilyn: Gary..I am not trying to get between you and your friend..But..If your friend called you to ask you how you are doing..You should appreciate it

Gary: You are getting between me and my friend

Marilyn: I thought you were stronger Gary..I never saw that side of you..You hung up on your best friend soon it will be me

Gary: What is wrong with you?

Marilyn: What is wrong with you?

Gary: You really want to know?

Marilyn: What did he say to you? Nothing

Gary: Nothing..But..Are you dead yet

Marilyn: What do you mean?

Gary: You heard me..He asked me..Are you dead yet?

Marilyn: Oh my god..Did he really say that?

Gary: You think I am making this up..You wanted to know..Now you know..He is my friend..I know how to treat my friends..I am not a child

Marilyn: I am sorry Gary..Thank you for standing up for me

Gary: This is nothing..Thomas is a good guy..But he plays too much sometimes

Marilyn: how did he know that I was tested positive?

Gary: I told him last night when he stopped by

Marilyn: You don't have to go around and tell everybody about my status

Gary: Not at all Marilyn..I wanted to talk to someone about the situation..He is the only person I told

Marilyn: You could have told me first

Gary: Tell you what?

Marilyn: You could have asked me if it is ok to tell him

Gary: I am sorry about that..But I needed to talk to someone..Your phone

Marilyn: What?

Gary: Your phone is ringing

Marilyn: I don't want to talk..Answer it for me and ask who it is

Gary: Hello

Kim: Hello..I did not know Marilyn's voice has gotten so deep

Gary: How are you Kim?

Marilyn: Let me talk to Kim

Kim: Hello

Marilyn: Hello stranger..How long ago since we talked

Kim: Two weeks..I just got here..I am not even home yet..I am still at the airport waiting for my luggage

Marilyn: How was the trip?

Kim: Great..A little tiring

Marilyn: How was the show?

Kim: It was great..I ended up signing with another company

Marilyn: Good for you

Kim: What is a matter?..You don't sound like yourself

Marilyn: I am fine..I am fine

Kim: Don't tell me that Marilyn..I know you..You don't sound happy..When you heard my voice after two weeks of hearing from me..You would have been very excited and happy

Marilyn: Well..Today is not the day

Kim: Is it me?..Did I do something to you?

Marilyn: C'mon Kim..Don't be ridiculous

Kim: What is it then?..Is it Gary?..He is trying to control you?..Why did he answer your phone?

Marilyn: No..Gary is fine..He is a sweetheart

Kim: I am going to stop by later to get to the bottom of this..See you later

Marilyn: Later when Kim?

Kim: You tell me when

Marilyn: Don't come now..I am going to take a nap

Kim: Are you pregnant?

Marilyn: No..I am not

Kim: Yes you are..See you after five..What do you want me to bring..I will get some food

Marilyn: Don't bother to bring anything..I am not in a mood to eat

Gary: I want to eat..Let her bring the food

Marilyn: Gary said bring the food

Kim: What does he want?

Marilyn: I don't know..What do you want Gary?

Kim: Does he like shrimp?

Marilyn: He does..Do you want shrimp babe?

Gary: Shrimp is fine

Marilyn: He said shrimp is fine

Kim: Ok..I will bring you your favorite cupcake

Marilyn: you don't have to go buy cupcake Kim

Kim: Marilyn..What is a matter?..You love cupcake..Something must be really wrong

Marilyn: I am fine..See you later Kim

Kim: Ok sweetie

_Later at Marilyn's place

Mindy: Do you want me to cook something baby?

Marilyn: No mom

Mindy: You've lost some weight Marilyn

Marilyn: How you figured mom

Mindy: Yes you have..Look at your pants..Look how loosed they are on you..You need to eat..You haven't been eating anything those two last weeks..And you are not telling anyone what is wrong

Marilyn: Mom please..Even if I tell you..What is it going to do?

Mindy: Do you want us to go to a movie tonight?

Marilyn: Mom..You need to save your strength

Mindy: We can go to a movie..I will be just fine..Let's make it our girl night

Marilyn: Thank you mom..But..Gary and Kim are coming here later

Mindy: Kim?..I thought she was in France for an event

Marilyn: She was..She came back today

Mindy: She must be tired

Marilyn: Kim is never tired..Beside she wants to come here to find out what is wrong with me

Mindy: See..I told you that you lost weight

Marilyn: Mom..She did not see me..I spoke with her on the phone and she thought that I was not happy..You know Kim..She worries always about the world..She thinks she can solve every mystery..She will not rest until she finds out what is wrong

Mindy: Well..She is concerned

Marilyn: I just think she is nosy..Kim likes to investigate everything

Mindy: She is my favorite amongst all your friends

Marilyn: Mom..Everybody is your favorite

Mindy: Do you want me to make something?

Marilyn: Kim will bring food

_ Meanwhile at Gary's parents

Gary's dad: Gary..How is school?

Gary: Great..I complete the clinical towards my credits

Gary's dad: Really?..That was quick..How was it?

Gary: It was very interesting..I had a chance to talk to a lot of people

Gary's dad: How is the young lady that you introduced to us..What's her name?

Gary: Her name is Marilyn dad..You don't ever remember people's names

Gary's dad: You are so right about that..This is my downfall..I just not good at names..You would think being in politics and having to deal with so many people will change that..To me it gets worse..I can't even remember my assistant's name

Gary: I know dad..Sometimes you even called me Steven instead of Gary

Gary's dad: I know..I know..How is Marilyn doing?

Gary: She is fine dad..Dad..I need to talk to you about something

Gary's dad: Go ahead..Shoot son..I know what it is

Gary: What is it dad?

Gary's dad: Dad..I need five hundred dollars to put a new fender in my car

Gary: You are wrong dad

Gary's dad: What is it then?

Gary: Maybe I should wait before telling you

Gary's dad: Since when you had secret for us..You were not raised that way

Gary: Dad..I know..But I am no longer a child

Gary's dad: What is it that you can tell me about?

Gary: Dad..You are going out right now..When you come back I will tell you

Gary's dad: I got time..There is no rush for me to leave..C'mon son..What is it?

Gary: Dad..You have to promise me that you are going to tell mom about it

Gary's dad: Ok..No problem at all..My mouth is sealed son..Go ahead shoot..Hold on a second..Let me get my coffee

Gary: Ok dad

Gary's dad: Is it good news or a bad news

Gary: Not a good news

Gary's dad: Someone is pregnant for you?

Gary: No dad..Marilyn was tested positive

Gary's dad: Marilyn..Marilyn..Your girlfriend?

Gary's dad: Positive of what? Drugs?..She does drugs?

Gary: No dad she does not do drugs

Gary's dad: Positive of what?

Gary: She is HIV positive dad

Gary's dad: Really?..How that happened..Promiscuous?

Gary: No dad..She was stuck with a dirty needle at her job

Gary's dad: I am sorry to hear that..What are you going to do about it

Gary: Well..I am going to give her all the support that she needs

Gary's dad: What do you mean? You do know this is an incurable disease..Right?

Gary: I know dad..I wrote a paper about it

Gary's dad: You are a smart young man..I know you are not going to risk your life by hanging around that woman

Gary: Dad..With all due respect..I have to say..Yes..I will hang around her a little bit longer

Gary's dad: You have to be smart in life Gary..I raised you to be smart..I sent you to great school..Now you are going t medical school..You need not be around that woman

Gary: dad..She is a young lady..She is a year younger than me

Gary's dad: What her illness has to do with you?

Gary: Dad..If you had an incurable disease..You would like to have my support..Right?

Gary's dad: Son..I am your dad..You don't know her

Gary: Dad..She is one of my best friends..How could I turn my back on her just because she is sick?

Gary's dad: I am trying to protect you Gary

Gary: I understand Dad..But..I want you to understand me as well..I will be completely safe

Gary's dad: what kind of relationship it's going to be..A friendship?

Gary: I don't know what you mean dad..She is my girlfriend

Gary's dad: You can't be careless..You are going our lives in danger as well

Gary: How so dad..Dad..You haven't done any research regarding that disease

Gary's dad: I don't need to do research regarding the disease..I know it is incurable..And it is contagious

Gary: Dad..You are very wrong..We can't turn our back on those who are infected by this disease

Gary's dad: So..I am going to tell you right now..If this is the way you chose to live..You will not be welcome at our house..I don't want you to come here and put our lives at risk

Gary: Dad..What do you mean?..You don't want to come home to see mom and my two little brothers

Gary's dad: You heard it right..This is a logic decision

Gary: Dad..I will agree with your logic decision..And I will adopt the humane decision..That is to stand with her..She has no one..Her dad passed away a year ago..Her mom has cancer..I can't turn my back on her dad..I just can't..Dad..You always encourage us to help others..To have compassion..What happened to the compassion you were preaching about?

Gary's dad: This is different Gary..Your life is at risk

Gary: It does not make any sense dad..You are a true politician dad..I will be a doctor one day..I have to deal with people who have contagious diseases

Gary's dad: This is different..It will be your job

Gary: Well..It is my duty as a human being to show compassion to her and not turn my back on her..To abandon her when she needs me the most is not in me

Gary's dad: Good luck son..I told you my position regarding this issue..You are not welcome in our home

Gary: Can I say goodbye to my two brothers?

Gary's dad: No you can't..They are doing homework now..So long

Gary: Mom is there?

Gary's dad: No..She will be home soon..I will tell her about your decision

Gary: So long dad..One day you will understand..Dad..I love my family..I just can't turn my back on her..I just can't..She needs me

Gary's dad: She needs you more than you need your family..Go ahead

_ Gary was devastated..He leaves his parents home with tears in his eyes..He walks slowly toward his car..He is asking himself the question over and over.. "Why did I mention that to my dad"..Then his phone rings..It is Marilyn calling him..Let's listen:

Gary: Hello

Marilyn: Hello..Gary..Are you ok?

Gary: I am fine

Marilyn: You don't sound fine..Were you crying?

Gary: No..Not at all..I am fine..How are you?

Marilyn: Something is wrong Gary?..Is it about me?

Gary: No..It's not about you..How is your mom doing?

Marilyn: You are trying to change the conversation..I know for sure something is wrong..I thought you were going to your parents' house

Gary: I was at my parents' house

Marilyn: Ok..Then why are you so upset?

Gary: I am fine Marilyn

Marilyn: Can you stop by a minute

Gary: Anything is wrong?

Marilyn: I just want to see you..Can you do that for me?

Gary: Just give me a few minutes and I will be there..Do you want anything to eat?

Marilyn: No..I am fine.,Just get here

Gary: See you soon..Who is talking in the background?

Marilyn: That's the TV..My mom is watching TV

Gary: Say hello to her for me

Marilyn: Gary..You are coming here..Right?

Gary: Yes

Marilyn: Why are you telling me to say hello to my mom..You will say hello to her when you get here

Gary: C'mon..You think I am not coming over because I asked you to say hello to your mom?

Marilyn: When you get here..You will say hello to her

Gary: See you soon

Marilyn: See you

_Meanwhile at Marilyn's home

Mindy: Someone is at the door

Marilyn: It must be Kim..She was on her way here

Mindy: I thought you said she got back from France today?

Marilyn: She did

Mindy: you should not have asked her to come here..She must be very tired for that long flight

Marilyn: Mom..I did not ask Kim to come here today..You know Kim..She wants to come here to find out what is wrong with me..I told you that already mom

Mindy: How since you know Kim?

Marilyn: I know Kim since elementary school mom..She is the same age as me..She is twenty three

Mindy: You are not twenty three yet

Marilyn: I will be twenty three in a month

Mindy: I know..What is the red thing on your shirt..Is your nose bleeding?

Marilyn: Oh my god..My nose is bleeding..Mom..Did you touch the blood?

Mindy: Yes I did

Marilyn: Why?

Mindy: There is nothing wrong with that..Who put bandages on your cut when you were a child?..Me

Marilyn: Mom..You play too much..You have to be more careful

Mindy: More careful about what?..You really think you are too old for me to take care of you?..Come here let me show you what to do to stop the bleeding

Marilyn: Mom..I am fine..I can take care of myself..Here mom

Mindy: What is that?

Marilyn: Alcohol swaps..Clean your hands

Mindy: Oh my god..You are becoming paranoid..It's not like you have an incurable disease or something..Even if you had an incurable and contagious disease..I will still take care of you..Where are you?..Who are you calling?

Marilyn: Hello Gary

Gary: Hello..How are you?

Marilyn: My nose is bleeding

Gary: Really?..You remember what the doctor said..The medication will cause nose bleed sometimes

Marilyn: I remember..You know what though

Gary: What?

Marilyn: My mom touched the blood

Gary: Why?

Marilyn: I did not know that my nose was bleeding..She saw the red on my shirt and she said..What is that on your shirt and she touched it

Gary: She will be fine..That should not be a problem..As long as she does not have any cuts in her fingers she will be ok..She washed her hands?

Marilyn: Yes..I gave her alcohol swaps to clean them..I was freaking out

Gary: You probably made her realize that something is wrong

Marilyn: No..Not really..I calmed down and told her to clean her hands..I want to check her fingers to see whether she has any cuts

Gary: No.Just leave it alone..She is fine..If you act too paranoid..She will realize something is wrong

Marilyn: I am going to ask her to see her nails..I usually do her nails for her

Mindy: Marilyn

Marilyn: Yes mom

Mindy: She is in the driveway

Marilyn: I heard her car

Gary: You are expecting someone?

Marilyn: Kim is stopping by

Gary: She is back from her trip from France?

Marilyn: She got back today..She is coming here because she suspects that something is wrong with me..What should I do?

Gary: About what?

Marilyn: Should I tell her about my medical condition

Gary: Well..It's up to you..She is your friend..If you feel like she is somebody you can trust..Do it then..She might be those types of people who will put you down and make you feel bad

Marilyn: Not at all..She is like a sister to me..I know Kim since elementary school..She is the nicest person..Very caring..The only thing about her she is nosey..If I don't tell her what is wrong..She will not rest..She will become annoying

Gary: She will transform into a private investigator

Marilyn: Private investigator?..Worse than that..Almost a stalker

Gary: Really?

Marilyn: That's how curious she is..I think I better off tell her

Gary: I think so too..It will be good to tell a good friend..You need that kind of support..Babe..I don't think that I should stop by right now..I should give you guys sometimes alone

Marilyn: You could come..She would be happy to see you

Gary: No..You say hello to her for me..I will see you later..The bleeding has stopped?

Marilyn: Yes it has..I read somewhere online..You just have to pinch your nose a little..Breathe through your mouth..And tilt your head back a little..I did that and it worked

Gary: Everything you need is online

Marilyn: Everything..Great resources

Gary: So..I will see you later..Say hello to Kim

Marilyn: I will

Gary: Is it ok if I ask you to say hello to your mom for me now?

Marilyn: Very funny mister..Yes it's ok since you are not coming over..I still want to know why you were sad

Gary: I had an argument with my dad..That's all

Marilyn: Was it about me?

Gary: No..Don't worry about

Marilyn: Kim is at the door..I have to go

Gary: Bye

Marilyn: Talk to you later

Gary: Why you sound sad..Your friend is there..Just be happy..Enjoy every day

Kim: Hello..Hello

Marilyn: Hello stranger

Kim: Oh my god..You look so good..Look at your hair..You lost so much weight

Marilyn: You look good..Not me..You are being sarcastic Kim?

Kim: C'mon girl..You know me better than that..I tell it the way it is..You really lost a lot of weight..Whatever diet you are on..It is working

Marilyn: I am not on any diet..My diet is life..I am going through so much..This is the name of my diet..Look at you..You are glowing..You change your hair color again?

Kim: Yes did..I only did it yesterday..You like it?

Marilyn: I love it

Kim: You want me to do it for you?

Marilyn: No..Not at this time Kim..I am not in the mood for that..I was even thinking of cutting my all my hair

Kim: How come?..You were never a fan of short hair

Marilyn: I was actually thinking of shaving it really low

Kim: Why would you do that?

Marilyn: It is getting thin..It does not look strong and healthy

Kim: You know what to do..Just put some avocado in it and voila

Marilyn: I don't know about that

Kim: You sound very depressed Marilyn..You know I am your girl..This is not the Marilyn that I know..You survived your dad's death..There is nothing that you cannot survive..You are my inspiration..I look up to you..Oh my god..Let me pop it for you

Marilyn: Oh my god..No..No..No..Don't do that Kim..Are you crazy?

Kim: What?..You have a little pimple on your upper arm..I was going to pop it for you..You know I like to that..Pop pimple on people..What is that about..I did it all the time for you..Why you jumped up and made such a big deal about it?

Marilyn: No Kim..You cannot do that..This is not safe for you..This is not safe for me

Kim: I was going to wash my hand right after..C'mon..Let me pop it for you..Don't be a chicken..Why are you crying Lyn?..Did I do something that offended you..Why are you crying?..I am so sorry..I am so sorry

Marilyn: You are fine..Don't be sorry..That's not you

Kim: What is happening?..You are making me cry..I don't even know what is wrong..You are crying..You are making me cry Marilyn..Oh my lord..What is happening to my sister?..You want to talk about it..Lyn..You know me and you have no secret for each other..Whenever something is wrong..Who do I call first ..Are you pregnant?..Come here let me dry your eyes

Marilyn: No..Don't do that

Kim: What is a matter..You don't want me to dry your eyes..You don't want to pop a small pimple on you..Why you think I am sick or something

Marilyn: It's not you Kim..It's me

Kim: What do you mean?

Marilyn: I am really sick

Kim: No..You are not baby..It's only in your mind..You worry so much..You are losing your mind..You stay in this house..You don't go anywhere..I know your dad passed away and mom is sick..But you can't just lie down and die because of that..Stop crying Lyn

Marilyn: Kim..I am sick..Trust me..I am very sick Kim..Next year at this time..I am not going to be in this world with you

Kim: Marilyn..You are talking crazy right now..Stop it or I will leave..Why are you doing this to me..Look at me..I am a mess..My makeup is all over my face..I did not come here to cry..You are fine..Shake it off Lyn..You are just depressed

Marilyn: Listen to me Kim..I wish I was just depressed..I would have happy if it was depression

Kim: What is wrong baby..Tell me..I am strong..Tell me what is wrong with you

Marilyn: Kim..I am tested positive

Kim: Lyn..You are crying..I can't hear a word you said

Marilyn: I am tested positive

Kim: Positive of what?

Marilyn: HIV

Kim: What?..What?..I am going to kill Mark..I am going to kill him..Are you serious?..He is dead..I don't care..You must be playing..I know you don't go anywhere..You were very faithful..This is why you broke up with him? He was cheating on you?..I don't care..I am going to prison

Marilyn: It's not Mark

Kim: It can't be Gary..You just started dating him

Marilyn: Kim..It's my job

Kim: What do you mean your job?

Mindy: Lyn..Where are you?

Marilyn: Let's go outside on the porch..My mom is up

Mindy: Where are you Lyn?

Marilyn: I am here mom

Mindy: Are you arguing with someone?

Marilyn: No mo..I am talking to Kim

Kim: Hello..Hello

Mindy: How are you Kim?

Kim: I am fine

Mindy: I am glad you came..Because your friend here needs a little shaking up..Shake her up a bit..She has not been herself lately..You look good Kim..Your eyes seem to be a bit red

Kim: It must be the allergy..I have watery eyes during this season

Marilyn: Let's go outside Kim

Kim: Ok

Mindy: You are running from me Lyn..I am not going to listen to your conversation

Marilyn: I did not say that mom..We just want to go outside mom

Mindy: No problem..Find out what's wrong with her for me ok Kim

Marilyn: Mom..Why are you so mean?

Mindy: I am not being mean at all..I am just concerned about you

Marilyn: I can't take this anymore

Mindy: You see what I am talking Kim..Why are you crying Lyn?..What did I say to make her so upset?

Kim: Well..She should be left alone..She might be dealing with some real difficult issues

Mindy: I understand that..But she could tell me

Marilyn: Let's go sit in your car Kim..My mom is too annoying

Mindy: You can stay here..Why in the car?..I'll leave you alone..It's time to take my shower anyway..See you later Kim

Kim: Ok

Marilyn: Let's go outside Kim..Close the door..Close the door..Thanks

Kim: When did you find out about it?

Marilyn: Last week

Kim: You look good..You don't look sick at all

Marilyn: I know..That will not last Kim..I can't afford those medications

Kim: I can help you

Marilyn: Kim..It's just too much..Gary said the same thing..I have to take so many different pills..At least fifteen different pills..They are all expensive..Some of them cost five hundred bucks..For only seven pills..There is no way

Kim: You don't have health insurance at your job..Do you?

Marilyn; No..I don't..And right now it's too late..Once I started to buy medication for the disease..The insurance company will step in to stop it..Because in the form they ask question about incurable diseases

Kim: I see..What about Gary..Does he have health coverage?

Marilyn: He does..But he is under his dad's policy

Kim: You think his dad could help?

Marilyn: No..Not at all..I suspect that his dad is pressuring him to stay away from me

Kim: How do you know that?

Marilyn: Today I called him..He did not sound like himself..He told me he had a fight with his dad..And he would not tell me what the fight was about

Kim: You think his dad is that kind of person?

Marilyn: To tell you the truth..I don't know his dad..But he is a politician..There an image he is trying to maintain

Kim: You are so right..Some politicians are so fake..Some of them become a senator just to get rich..Making money from the lobbyists..It's not always about the people who put them in office

Marilyn: I know

Kim: But..No matter what..I will stand with you..I am with you

Marilyn: Thank you Kim

Kim: Have you told any of the other girls?

Marilyn: I think it's still too early..I don't want them to worry about me..There is nothing they can really do..All this happen at such a bad time..I am trying to help my mom battle the cancer..Now this

Kim: Don't start talking like that..You are going to make me cry..Now it's time for us to fight..You have to survive this disease

Marilyn: I know..Gary told me that his goal is to become a researcher..In order to find a cure for this disease

Kim: That's nice of him..He must be a very good person

Marilyn: He is..He has been so supportive since I found out about my status..He wants to find a cure

Kim: Really?..Is he that smart?

Marilyn: He is smart and very creative..He thinks out of the box..I won't be surprised if he found a cure for this disease

Kim: Wow..That would be amazing

_Meanwhile Gary and Thomas are having a conversation

Thomas: Gary..You can just come in her without knocking

Gary: Well lock the door Tom

Thomas: I could have had a girl with me here

Gary: Well..That would not have been the first time

Thomas: What are you up to?..What brought you here..You usually don't come to my place..Even when I invite you don't come

Gary: Well..Your place is usually like a hording house..It does not look too bad today..What is the occasion?

Thomas: There is no occasion..I am lying..I expect that new girl to stop by later

Gary: I knew you were up to something..Your room is never that clean

Thomas: Whatever man..Are you ready for the exams?

Gary: I think so

Thomas: You are always ready..Smart guy

Gary: You are probably smarter than me Thomas

Thomas: You are the one with all the A's..All I have it's B's

Gary: You party too much Tom..Imagine if you were spending time in your books

Thomas: I love that way..I can't live without the ladies..Talking about the ladies..How is Marilyn doing?

Gary: She is fine..I wanted to talk to you..To ask you what you think

Thomas: About what?..You being with her?..I told you already..I respect your decision

Gary: Not that Tom..I have been thinking some crazy thoughts lately

Thomas: Like what?

Gary: You know I need to find a way to help Marilyn

Thomas: What do you mean?

Gary: To help her..You know the medications are very expensive..And she does not have health coverage

Marilyn: How would you be able to help her?

Gary: I come up with an unusual idea

Thomas: What is it?..You are going to rob some pharmacies..And steal medications..You will soon be in the news as the pharmacy bandit

Gary: Very funny Thomas..By the way..Did I tell you?..I want to join a research team after my graduation

Thomas: Really?

Gary: Yes

Thomas: I see why..That's a great idea..You will be focusing on finding a cure for the HIV virus

Gary: Definitely

Thomas: You have to be very careful Gary..This is big business..An entire industry is built on that illness

Gary: I know..I understand..Billion dollar companies are created..Medications have to sell..Billion dollars are being made every day because of this disease

Thomas: I know..So..Finding a cure may not sit well with those companies

Gary: I even read an article that this disease was created in laboratories just to boost countries' economy

Thomas: I read that article as well

Gary: But think about it..Too many people died already..Losing one person is too many for that person's love ones..I don't mind working to find a solution to that problem..Not only that Marilyn is infected..The disease hit home..So..I think this is the time for me to get involved and try to save her life..I have no choice..I promised her that I will stand with her and help her fight the battle..So this is one aspect of the battle..But first..You remember I told you that I came up with an unusual idea..Right?

Thomas: Well..All your ideas are unusual Gary..You are my only genius friend..This is why I tolerate you

Gary: Thank you..You are my only playboy friend..This is why I tolerate you..What is the unusual idea?

Gary: Don't be shocked

Thomas: Be shocked about your ideas?..Never..I know you already..If it's not unusual it's not from Gary..What is it already?

Gary: Well..Marilyn does not have health coverage..And I do..I could share my health coverage with her

Thomas: How you are going to do that Gary?

Gary: I could purchase the medications for her

Thomas: How is that is going to be possible..I know you are a genius and all..But..How you are going to purchase medications for her with under your dad's policy

Gary: Simple

Thomas: Shoot..Let me hear it

Gary: Simple my friend..All I have to do is to be infected..Then I will be able to share my medications with her..Why you are not talking?

Thomas: I am still trying to process what you just said..Did you say you have to get infected?

Gary: You heard me right

Thomas: Infected with what?

Gary: Infected with the HIV virus

Thomas: This brilliant..Creative approach..But the most risky thing I heard

Gary: No..It is not the most risky..People go to war every day..Young men are sent to wars to defend and fight for people they don't even know..They risk of getting shot and getting killed by doing so..In fact a lot of them died in every war..Which do you think is more risky?

Thomas: They are both risky..You would in fact inject yourself with the virus in order to buy medications and share them with Marilyn

Gary: Yes..This is what I have to do..Otherwise she will die

Thomas: My brother..You have the biggest heart..I thought I was a man..You are the bravest man I have ever seen..I have so much respect for you..In a million years something like that would never cross my mind..You open my eyes..You open my heart

Gary: You know what they say..Only with love you can teach love

Thomas: My friend..It is very risky

Gary: I know..I will have access to the best medications that are out there..And Marilyn will too..I have to do something..I have to put myself as a shield between her and the disease

Thomas: This is exactly what you are doing..Using yourself as a shield between you and the disease..Wow..I am in shock..Is this just a thought..Or this is something that

Gary: Let me stop you Tom..I thought this over and over from the day I realized she could not afford the medications and the outcome would be death

Thomas: You know you might die..Because the virus affects different people differently

Gary: I know..But this is the risk I must take

Thomas: Is she aware of your decision?

Gary: No..Not at all..She would be completely against it

Thomas: How you intend to get infected?

Gary: I want to do it through her..So I can get the same strain she has

Thomas: It's not going to be easy

Gary: I know..She is so careful..She does not even want me to kiss her on the lips..During sex she insists that I use two set of protections..But I will find a way

_Meanwhile at Marilyn's house

Kim: Your mom does not know about it

Marilyn: No..She doesn't..C'mon Kim..You know how my mom is..She worries about everything..She would not survive if she found out about something like this

Kim: How are you going to keep it secret from her?

Marilyn: I have to Kim..I have no choice

Kim: I want you to know..We will find a way..You are not going to die..It is just a disease like any other diseases..As long to treat it..You will be fine

Marilyn: Treating it is the key

_A couple months later- Kim is having a dinner party to celebrate her little sister going away for a job overseas. Words had gone around pretty quick regarding Marilyn's medical condition..One friend tells one friend..The other friend tells the next and before you know it the whole community knows..Kim invites Marilyn to the party..She always encourages Marilyn to try to live a normal live..Kim is a great friend to Marilyn..They are on the phone..Let's listen:

Kim: Lyn..You know the party is tonight..Right

Marilyn: Is it?

Kim: C'mon Lyn..Don't is it me

Marilyn: I know..I am just messing with you

Kim: You better be

Marilyn: Is it too late to call out

Kim: Yes it is..How are you feeling..You can make it

Marilyn: I am feeling fine..I should be able to make it..Hopefully my nose will not bleed

Kim: Does it bleed every day?

Marilyn: No..Not every day..It is caused by the medications

Kim: I know..You should not worry..It won't happen

Marilyn: At what time I should be there

Kim: You guys should come a little earlier if you want..But everything starts at nine o'clock

Marilyn: Gary will not be able to make it..I am coming alone..Is that ok?..It's not a couples party..Is it?

Kim: No..Not at all..My sisters are coming..You met Dionne right?

Marilyn: Of course..I met Dionne

Kim: Have you met Alexandra?

Marilyn: Kim what is a matter with you..You forgot I know you since elementary school..I met all your four sisters..You forgot all of us used to go to the movies and try to snick into another room to see another movie

Kim: I know..I know..Why Gary is not coming?..He is always avoiding coming to my place..I don't eat people

Marilyn: He has to study tonight..He has exams coming up

Kim: You will be able to drive..Right?

Marilyn: Kim..I am not dead yet..I might die..But I am still alive..Of course I can drive

Kim: Very funny Lyn..I never said you were dead..So I will see you tonight..Come a little earlier..So we can talk a bit before everybody arrives

Marilyn: No problem my dear

Kim: See you later

Mindy: Who was on the phone?

Marilyn: That was Kim mom

Mindy: She is having a party?

Marilyn: Yes..Tonight

Mindy: That's her birthday?

Marilyn: No..Her sister is leaving the country for work..So..She is having a dinner party for her

Mindy: Are you going?

Marilyn: Yes mom

Mindy: Very nice..You've been a little happier lately..They only thing you need to work on now

Marilyn: What is it mom?

Mindy: You need to gain some weight..You've lost too much weight lately

Marilyn: Mom please..Enough already

Mindy: What did I do baby?..I am your mom..I have to tell you those things

Marilyn: Mom..I would rather you don't..You are always judging me..Scrutinize me

Mindy: Not at all..Don't be so sensitive

Marilyn: I am not sensitive mom..You are just annoying

Mindy: How could you call your mom annoying?

Marilyn: You are mom

Mindy: When I was growing up..If I had ever called my mom annoying..You know what would happen to me

Marilyn: I don't know..What?

Mindy: I would be dead..Twice..My mom would kill me..Then when my dad gets home he would kill me again

Marilyn: Grandpa and grandma were the sweetest people..Why you are accusing them of being killers

Mindy: Well..You are their grand kid..They were not that nice to me when I was growing up..They were not abusive..They never hit me..But..They were very strict..I could not get away with anything..I was surprised when they told me that I was too strict with you

Marilyn: Well mom..Kids these days don't get killed for calling their mom annoying

Mindy: I can see that

Marilyn: Because moms are just annoying..Nosy..Always trying to find out what is going on

Mindy: Don't worry..When you have your own kids..You will know what being annoying is like

Marilyn: Not anytime soon anyway..If ever

Mindy: Don't if ever me..At some point I want to see my grandchildren

Marilyn: well too bad mom..This is what you get for being annoying

Mindy: I can't believe my sweet little girl can talk to me this way

Marilyn: Mom..Do you want something to eat?

Mindy: Not really..Make me some cereal

Marilyn: You want me to slice banana in it?

Mindy: No..Just plain

_Later at the party at Kim's house

Marilyn: Kim

Kim: Yes

Marilyn: Why don't you answer your phone Kim?

Kim: I am sorry honey..I was in the kitchen and the phone was in the living room

Marilyn: From the time I know you..You never like to answer your phone

Kim: Well.. Those were the time where boys would try to call me non-stop..Where are you?

Marilyn: I am in your driveway..I am calling you to open the door

Kim: Come already

Marilyn: Hi

Kim: You look so good

Marilyn: Are you sure the party is today?

Kim: Why?

Marilyn: Nobody is here

Kim: It's still early

Marilyn: What were you doing? I see you with gloves on

Kim: I was in the kitchen

Marilyn: I thought you were ordering the food

Kim: The Gourmet is in charge of the food..I was making a cocktail that Alex likes

Marilyn: Who is Alex?

Kim: Alex is my new date..I met him while I was I Paris

Marilyn: He lives here in the United States?

Kim: He has family here but he works in France..He is coming just for the dinner..He is living to Paris in a couple of days

Marilyn: I think it's that time..I heard someone in the driveway

Kim: This is the people from Gourmet..Bringing the food

Marilyn: That's kind of late..Isn't it?

Kim: I wanted them to bring it at this time..I wanted it to be very hot..You like the way I set the table?

Marilyn: that's pretty neat..But it seems longer than your table

Kim: I bought another table..There are two tables there

Marilyn: That's huge

Kim: We are expecting close to forty people

Marilyn: You will be able to sit all forty?

Kim: Definitely..There is a cocktails room

Marilyn: That's nice

_Later during the party

Kim: Hello everyone I want to introduce you to my sisters Alexandra and Dionne

Janelle: Hello guys..I met Alexandra

Alexandra: I met Janelle before

_During the sitting..Marilyn sits at a spot..The two people on either sides of got up and change seat..There were two empty seats on both sides of her..No one wanted to sit next to her..Kim realized that and quickly took action

Kim: Come here Lyn..Come sit next to me..You know you have to be near me..What were you doing all the way over there?..You know you have to me near me

Marilyn: I know

_Everything was fine..The guests were enjoying the food and having nice conversations..Kim moved off the table for short while..She was talking on the phone and had retreated to another section of the house that was less noisy..Marilyn was talking to a Candice a young lady that went to high School with..She was also a good friend of Alexandra..All hails broke loose in the dining room when Candice made a simple remark

Candace: Your nose is bleeding

Marilyn: My nose?

Candace: Yes..Your nose is bleeding

Marilyn: Oh my god

_Following Candace's remark..Panic sets in the room..Everyone is running every which way to get away from Marilyn as quick as possible..Marilyn gets up to look for a restroom..Everywhere she goes the crowd screams and moves away like a wave..She is not chasing the people but it seems so..Because she wants to get to the restroom as quick as possible..But she is not sure where to find one..She tries to ask..Please where is the restroom she says..The lady answers..Get away from me..I don't know..She turns to go the other direction..Another lady says..Don't even try it coming this way..By then Kim is off the phone and she hears the screaming and commotion in the dining area..She makes her way there..And sees Marilyn trying to run every which way..People are scattering..She tries to go pass Alex..He pushes her away with a chair..So hard that Kim has to extend her arms to catch Marilyn and prevent her from falling

Kim: What's going on Lyn?

Marilyn: My nose is bleeding..My nose

Kim: It's ok..It's ok..You will be fine

Marilyn: I am so sorry..There is blood on the floor

Kim: Don't you worry about that..I will have it cleaned up..Let me take you to the restroom

Marilyn: You have blood on your clothes

Kim: Don't worry about it..I will change clothes..Take out this shirt..You have blood stand on it..Let me give you another one

Marilyn: Thank you so much Kim

Kim: Don't worry about it

Marilyn: I am so sorry I upset the people at the party

Kim: Don't worry about the party..A party is just a party..Your health is more important..Take your time take care of yourself..I have to talk to Alex

Kim: Sorry everyone..My friend had a little incident..Alex..Can I talk to you for a minute?

Alex: What is it darling?

Kim: I should ask you that question..What is it with you?

Alex: Why?

Kim: I saw you pushing my friend away with a chair

Alex: You saw that?..I was concerned..Just like everyone else

Kim: There was no call for it..It's unacceptable..If I did not catch her she would have ended up on the floor

Alex: I had no choice

Kim: Yes you had a choice..You had a choice to behave like a decent human being and you chose to behave like an animal

Alex: I had no choice..I heard she is infected with a deadly disease

Kim: So what..It could have been you..She is only human

Alex: I had no choice but to protect myself Kim

Kim: Well..Right now you only have one choice..It is for you to leave my home

Alex: What do you mean?

Kim: I mean get out now

Beatrice: What is happening Kim?

Kim: Stay out of it Beatrice..Leave now

Alex: I don't understand

Kim: That's the point..People like you will never understand

Alex: You are making a terrible mistake Kim

Kim: The terrible mistake I made it already..It was to think that you are a decent human being

Alex: can we go outside and talk about it

Kim: You said everything you had to say the way you pushed her away with the chair..And I saw all that I needed to see about you..Get out please

Alex: I will call you tomorrow when you calm down

Kim: You need to call a place where they are offering classes about being more humane to others..Don't waste your time calling me

_Following those words Alex gathered himself and made his way through the small crowd..Meanwhile

Gary: Thomas..Have you gone over the neurology yet?

Thomas: I will leave it last..It's strange you stay so long without calling Marilyn

Gary: You right about that..I should call her and see how she is doing..Let me call her

Kim: Lyn..Your phone is ringing

Marilyn: Answer it for me

Kim: Are you sure?

Marilyn: C'mon Kim..What do you mean?..Only Gary calls me

Kim: Hello

Gary: Hello..Lyn?

Kim: No..It's not Lyn

Gary: Kim..How are you?

Kim: I am fine..Marilyn is in the restroom..She had a little incident she asked me to answer the phone for her

Gary: What happened?

Kim: She is ok..Her nose was bleeding

Gary: Really?..She has nose bleeds quite often..You need me to come over

Kim: She is fine..We handle it

Gary: Did the bleeding stop?

Kim: Lyn..Did it stop?

Marilyn: Yes..I am holding it a little longer just for precaution

Kim: Yes..The bleeding stopped

Gary: Ok..I will call her back later..In thirty minutes or so

Kim: Ok Gary..I will talk to you soon

Gary: Ok

Kim: Let me com in there..How are you?..Are you ok?

Marilyn: I am fine..I am sorry about the inconvenience

Kim: Don't be sorry..You are at my house..My house is yours Lyn..What happened to your leg..You have a bruise there

Marilyn: I know..One of the women out there kicked me when I was moving around trying to find the restroom..I guess I was coming too close to her

Kim: Who did that?

Marilyn: I can't tell you..I was being pushed left and right

Kim: Hold on..Let me ask my sister..Alexandra..Come here..Can you come for a minute

Alexandra: What's up?

Kim: Did you see who kicked Lyn in the leg..Look at her leg..She has a bruise there

Alexandra: I could not tell you exactly..People were just acting so childish

Kim: This is not being childish..This is just ignorant and inhumane..I am going to do smoothing about it

Marilyn: Never mind Kim..It's ok..I am alive..I did not die..You would not find the person who did it

Kim: I know..Since I can't find the person..I am going to handle it my way

Alexandra: What are you going to do?

Kim: Wait and see..Everybody..May I have your attention please..We had an incident here..My friend had a nose bleed..I apologized for the inconvenience..Many of you have acted in a deplorable manner..Inhumane manner to say it right..Lyn is like a sister to me..I have known her since elementary school..We are all human beings here..We are all susceptible to be affected by diseases..Those diseases don't fall on trees..They affect human beings..Therefore..Your behavior tonight was disappointing to me..She was pushed by a chair..She was kicked by a woman..She has a bruise on her leg as a result of the kicking.. She could not remember who did the kicking..Since she cannot remember who did it..I don't think it's fair to her nor to my standard as a human being to let such person be inside my home any longer..Therefore..I will ask everybody to leave..The party is basically over..I appreciate your effort of coming..Now it is the time for me to spend some quiet time with my friend to make her understand that not all human beings behave in such manner..Those of you who did not participate in the pushing and kicking..I apologize to you..Thank you for coming

_Five minutes later..Kim her two sisters and Marilyn were the only ones there..Marilyn was still upset about the incident..Especially the way she was treated by the other guests..She had tears in her eyes

Marilyn: I think I should leave Kim

Kim: You are ok?..You will be able to drive?

Marilyn: Yes..Definitely..I feel fine

Kim: Don't cry..People are mostly mean..You need to build a thick skin..People will go out of their way to try to make you uncomfortable..They will not think one second about a way to make someone's life better but they will spend hours..Days trying to make someone's life miserable..You have to be mentally strong..Because the world is filled of those evil people..You should stay here when you are less upset you can leave

Kim: I am fine Kim..I think I can go now

Kim: Are you sure?

Marilyn: I think so..Where did I put my bag?

Kim: I put it in my room for you..Come..It's in my room

Marilyn: Thank you Kim

Kim: You are welcome..Let me walk you out..Call me ok..Let me know how you are doing

Marilyn: Thank you Kim..I will

Kim: Your car looks so clean

Marilyn: Gary took it to the carwash for me..He is allergic to dirty car..See you later

Kim: Call me when you get home

Marilyn: Ok..I will..Thank you for everything

Kim: You are welcome

_Marilyn drives home..She cries the whole time she is driving..She is hurt really bad by the way she was treated tonight..She is such a compassionate person..She did not expect to be treated in such a way by others..She learned the hard way about the nature of human beings..She gets home..She tries to be as quiet as she can be to not wake up her mom..She is in no condition to have a conversation with her mom..She does not want her mom to see she is crying..She quietly goes into her room and closes the door..She takes off her shoes and lies in her bed..Five minutes later..Someone pushes the door open..She opens her eyes..She does not believe it..Let's listen:

Marilyn: Dad?..Dad?..Is that you?

Marilyn's Dad: Yes it's me baby

Marilyn: Oh my god..Am I dreaming?

Marilyn's Dad: No you are not dreaming..It's me..I see that you are hurt really bad..So I come here to console you

Marilyn: Dad..I thought you were dead

Marilyn's Dad: We don't die..We transition into a new existence..The so called dead people are not allowed to interfere with those who have not yet reached the transition stage..But we see you guys..Sometimes it is so hard to watch our love ones suffer and there is nothing we are allowed to do about it

Marilyn: Dad..You are wearing a white shirt..You never like white shirt

Marilyn's Dad: Well..That's the color we all wear after the transition..This is an exception they made to allow me to come and see you..I have been waiting for you for a while..I could not talk to you at the party

Marilyn: Dad..You know I am sick?

Marilyn's Dad: Yes I know my love..This is why I am here..To tell you that everything is going to be ok..Don't cry..Don't cry..I want you to be a strong girl..I want you to be brave..I want you to be an inspiration to those affected by this disease..I want you to talk to young adult about the disease..I also want you to educate people about the disease..So they don't treat people the way you were treated tonight

Marilyn: Dad..You know something

Marilyn's Dad: What baby?

Marilyn: Mom is sick

Marilyn's Dad: I know..She has cancer..Mom will be fine..I would love to talk to her but I am not allowed..Tell mom stop burning her hand..The young man you are friend with

Marilyn: Gary?

Marilyn's Dad: Yes Gary

Marilyn: He is not my friend dad..He is my boyfriend

Marilyn's Dad: He is a very good young man..He will stand with you..He will fight the battle with you through the end..I just want you to know that you are not alone..I am here with you..I am watching over you..Just be strong..Everybody has different tests..Different obstacles..They have to go through in life..This is your obstacle..Therefore..Be strong

Marilyn: But dad..Sometimes I feel overwhelmed..I have to take care of mom..And now I have to battle this illness..I wish you were here with us

Marilyn's Dad: I am here with you..I have to leave now

Marilyn: Dad..What am I going to do?..Don't go yet dad..Dad..I am going to die

Marilyn's Dad: No you are not..Trust me..I will see my grandchild

Marilyn: Dad..You made me smile

Marilyn's Dad: I want you to smile..It's nothing but another illness..You will be fine

Marilyn: Thank you dad

Marilyn's Dad: Bye..I will be around..Say hello to mom for me

Marilyn: Should I tell mom you were here?

Marilyn's Dad: Yes you can..I don't know if she is going to believe you

Marilyn: I know..Dad..Dad..Where did you go

Mindy: Marilyn..Who are you talking to?

Marilyn: Mom?

Mindy: I heard you talking..Who was that?..Were you on the phone?

Marilyn: I was not on the phone mom

Mindy: Your room feels so cold

Marilyn: You feel cold

Mindy: I smell your dada cologne in here..You've been using his cologne Lyn

Marilyn: No mom..I was just talking to dad..He said hello..He said you are going to be ok..He said stop burning your hand

Mindy: He said what?

Marilyn: He told me to tell you..To stop burning your hand

Mindy: Oh my god..Oh my god..How did he know that?

Marilyn: Did you burn your hand mom?

Mindy: Yes..I did last week..While I was making breakfast..I did not tell you about it..No one knows about that

Marilyn: He said that he is here with us

Mindy: He must be..I believe you..Oh my god..I never believed in those things before..How does he look?

Marilyn: He looks the same

Mindy: What was he wearing?

Marilyn: He had a white shirt on

Mindy: Really?

Marilyn: Yes..I am so happy..I feel so good

Mindy: You needed that..You should have taken a picture for me

Marilyn: C'mon mom..You don't think of thing like that in the moment.. It's almost like he was controlling my mind..I did not move the whole time he was talking to me..They have the power to immobilize you..He said we don't die..After this life..We transition into another life

Mindy: So..There is life after death?

Marilyn: Yes mom..There is no death dad said..We don't die

Mindy: Oh my god..This is too much for me

Marilyn: We just transition to another life..Mom..Why you are crying?

Mindy: I still can smell his cologne in here

Marilyn: Mom..He is ok..He looks good

Mindy: When did he say that he is coming back?

Marilyn: He did not say mom..He said they did not allow him to come visit you..He said he only came because I was really hurt..They made an exception for him to come

Mindy: Who are they? Did you ask him?

Marilyn: I did not mom..I was not in my right mind..First of all that's the biggest shock in life..To see a love one who has passed away

Mindy: I know..I don't think I would be able to handle that

Marilyn: This is why he does not want to visit you

Mindy: I would love to see him one more time

Marilyn: I was so happy to see him..I feel so good right now..I don't feel down anymore

Mindy: How did he get in the room?

Marilyn: He pushed the door open

_The next morning..Gary is talking with his friend Thomas..Let's listen:

Thomas: You look really tired today Gary

Gary: It's not just a look..I am in fact very tired..More so mentally

Thomas: Is it school?..Or is it Marilyn situation

Gary: I would say both

Thomas: I think you should take the semester off in order to get things figure out

Gary: No..I can't do that my friend..I am in a race right now..I have to join the research team..My focus is to find a cure for that disease

Thomas: I understand that..But if you get exhausted or have a mental breakdown..That won't help either

Gary: I understand..Good point you made there Thomas

Thomas: I always make good point

Gary: I don't know about that..Certainly not when you are talking with me

Thomas: Really?..How come I am always the one you asked for advice?

Gary: Well..I want to pick your brain to see what you think about the subject so I can do the opposite

Thomas: Really?

Gary: Look at your face..I got you..Didn't it?..I am only kidding..You are one of the smartest guys I know..This is why you are my best buddy

Thomas: I knew you were kidding..You would be lost without my intellectual guidance

Gary: I never said that..Don't push it..Today I have to go and check the result of my test

Thomas: What test would that be?

Gary: The HIV test

Thomas: For what?

Gary: I have been trying to get infected

Thomas: You have already started that campaign?

Gary: Yes

Thomas: What method you have been using?

Gary: I had sexual encounter with Marilyn and I removed the condom every time

Thomas: You did?..She does not realize it?

Gary: No..Not at all..So..Today I am going to check the result..Hopping it is positive

Thomas: This is so strange..Someone hoping his HIV test to be positive..Never heard of something like that..You are the bravest man I have ever seen

Gary: Ok..I am going to the medical center to check the result..I will let you know

Thomas: No problem

_Gary then gets in his car and drives to the medical center to get the result of the test..Ten minutes later..He arrives at the center..Let's listen:

Gary: Good morning

Nurse: Good morning..How can I help you?

Gary: I am here for the result of my test

Nurse: What is your name please?

Gary: Gary

Nurse: Gary..Gary..I remember you..Just hold on one second please

Gary: Thank you

Nurse: Here it is..It's inside the envelop

Gary: Thank you

Nurse: Good luck

_Gary quickly opens the envelop while standing in front of the nurses' station

Gary: Man..Negative again?

Nurse: You said negative..Right?

Gary: Yes..It's disappointing

Nurse: Aren't negative supposed to be a good thing?

Gary: Well..Not really

Nurse: Are you suicidal?

Gary: No..I am not

Nurse: Well..Do you know..This disease can kill you?

Gary: Yes..I know that

Nurse: Do you know that there is no cure for it?

Gary: I am aware of that as well

Nurse: Well..Why you wish you were positive?

Gary: Because I want to help my girlfriend

Nurse: How can you help someone by being HIV positive?

Gary: It's a long story

Nurse: Tell me about it..You don't have to go in details..Let me know how you might help her by being positive

Gary: She does not have health insurance..So..Since I have insurance through my dad's policy..If I am positive I will be able to share my medicines with her..And prevent her from dying

Nurse: Why would you do that?..It is too risky

Gary: Without risk you can never accomplish something meaningful

Nurse: This is your life you are putting at risk..It's different

Gary: Let me ask you a question..Can I?

Nurse: Go ahead

Gary: If you had a close family member who needed a kidney..You would not give he or she one of your kidneys?

Nurse: Sure..As long that I am a match

Gary: Well.. It is the same thing

Nurse: I beg to differ..Donating an organ and infecting yourself with a deadly disease are two different things

Gary: You can die during surgery right?

Nurse: Of course..People die every day during surgery

Gary: Thank you..Therefore, there are risks in both situations..Are there not?

Nurse: I know..I know..That's a very brave thing you are doing..I would not advise anyone to do such a thing..You know you can get really sick..And even die way before her

Gary: I am aware of that..The disease affects every patient differently

Nurse: That's right..The virus can act very aggressive in your system and destroy your immune system in no time..Then you would have full blown aids

Gary: I understand all that..I did a lot of research..But I promised her that I will fight the battle with her..I can't abandon her..I am the only one she has..This is the only way for her to get access to the right medicines..That will give her a chance to survive

Nurse: I am sorry..I did not mean to get you upset..I saw tears in your eyes

Gary: Yes..Talking about it gets me upset..Because she is such a wonderful young lady..Full of life..Hoping to become a doctor one day..Those tears are not tears of weakness..I am prepared to die along the way fighting the battle with her..By doing so..Engaging into the battle..I will give her a chance to live one more day..One more week..One more month..And hopefully one more year

Nurse: You are a wonderful young man..With the biggest heart I have ever seen

Gary: What did your parents think of all this?

Nurse: My parents don't know that I am doing this

Gary: My dad already stops talking with me..Not only that..He forbids me from coming to the house because I did not break up with my girlfriend

Nurse: Since you can't go back home..Where do you stay?

Gary: I had my own apartment

Nurse: Ok..You are in school right?

Gary: I am in medical school

Nurse: How do you pay for the apartment?

Gary: My parents pay for it

Nurse: Your dad might stop paying for it

Gary: He would not do that..If he does..My mom would pay it for me..He is only mad because he feels that I am putting my life in danger to save someone else's life

Nurse: I wish you luck..I hope god protects you..Because you are doing a very good deed..You are trying your best to save her life

Gary: Thank you

Nurse: One final question..I would like to ask you

Gary: Go ahead

Nurse: How does your girlfriend feel about that?

Gary: About me infecting myself?

Nurse: Yes

Gary: She does not know about it..She would have opposed to it..Therefore..I keep it a secret

Nurse: Good luck..I will pray for you..Let me know how you are doing..If you need anything..Feel free to contact me..Here's my card

Gary: Thank you..Hopefully next time I will be positive

Nurse: I still can't wish that for you..Your phone is ringing

Gary: Yes..Thank you

Thomas: Gary..Why you took so long to answer the phone

Gary: Is it a crime..And last time I checked..This phone was mine

Thomas: Don't get smart with me..What happened..What is the result?

Gary: Not good man..Disappointing..It's negative again

Thomas: Disappointing?..Are you kidding..I support what you are doing..But at the same time..As a friend and a brother..I just don't like it..The reason is..What if you started to get really sick and die?

Gary: Well..Everybody has to die at one point..I am afraid to die..It is part of life

Thomas: I know all that..But you are a long life to live..Why jeopardize it

Gary: Are we going to have that conversation again?

Thomas: I don't mean to bother you at all..I just want you to know how I feel about it

Gary: I hear how you feel Thomas..But it is more than that to me..Getting myself infected to me it's a humane duty..Let me ask you a quick question if you don't mind

Thomas: Yes..I don't mind at all

Gary: Let's say you were diving with a partner..Very far down below..She is having problem with her oxygen tank..And there is no way she will make it to the surface without some oxygen..You would not share your oxygen with her

Thomas: Of course I would

Gary: Why would you do it?

Thomas: It's simple..To give her a chance to live

Gary: Exactly..This is the reason I am doing this for Marilyn..Just to give her a chance to live..You know well by removing the oxygen from your mouth and giving it to her..You are putting your life at risk..Right?..Because you need the oxygen to survive

Thomas: Yes..I understand..That was a great analogy..I get it

Gary: Let me ask you one more question

Thomas: What is it today?..Questions day?

Gary: No..I am trying to unlock the door of your heart that leads to the humane area

Thomas: Very funny Gary..Go ahead..Ask the question already

Gary: Let say you had ten cars park in your driveway..And you see a person who does not have a car to go to work and make a living..Would you give him one of your cars?

Thomas: What kind of car we are talking about Gary?

Gary: It does not matter a car is a car..A car can only do one thing..Taking you somewhere

Thomas: You know I am a car crazy guy..I would have to take a good look at which one

Gary: C'mon Thomas..Your humane duty should overshadow your love for material things..A car is at the end of the day pieces of metal

Thomas: I know Gary..I was just messing with you..Of course I will give away one

Gary: My point your duty to help others should always come first..This is the only way you and I can make the world a better place..This is not for no reason you want to become a surgeon..It is simply to help people

Thomas: Don't talk so fast my brother..I want to be a surgeon..So I could cut people and not go to jail for it

Gary: Very funny Thomas..I heard that joke before

Thomas: Well..It is not a joke to me..That's really the way I feel

Gary: I know..You are a born assassin

Thomas: Assassin is too fancy..I am a born killer

Gary: Whatever killer..Get off my phone..You are killing my battery

Thomas: You called me

Gary: Wrong..You called me..You were so anxious to know whether I am going to die from that disease

Thomas: You right..I just have no heart to do it..I will let the disease do it

Gary: I already know..Talk to you later buddy..I am going to call Marilyn and see how she is doing

Thomas: Later brother..Today is Friday..You are stopping by at the frat house

Gary: I am not sure about that..I might spend sometimes with Marilyn instead

Thomas: No problem..If you choose to stop by..I will be there until around midnight..Then I will be at the school launch area

Gary: What is happening there?

Thomas: I will go there to do some reading

Gary: Why don't you stay in your room and read

Thomas: You are lucky Gary..You have your own apartment..On Fridays..My roommate Kevin always has at least two girls in the room with him

Gary: I know Kevin..You and Kevin are a good match..I don't which one of you will win player of the year award

Thomas: You can't compare me to Kevin..He sleeps with at least a dozen different girls in a week

Gary: That sounds just like you

Thomas: C'mon Gary..I am better than that

Gary: Yeah right..You are better..Later brother..Marilyn is on the other line

Thomas: Peace

Marilyn: Hello..Who you were talking to on the phone

Thomas: How do you know I was talking to someone?

Marilyn: Babe..You know when you are talking to someone the phone makes a longer sound

Gary: I never realized that

Marilyn: Of course babe..You are living under a rock?

Gary: I am in term of technology..Not technology in a whole..I am not a phone crazy guy

Marilyn: You go and say that to my friends

Gary: Some people change their phone very six months

Marilyn: A new phone will come out in two months..My friends go crazy

Gary: What they don't understand..Sometimes..It's only one little feature that is added to the phone..It's exactly the same product..People spend two nights in line in front of the store waiting for it

Marilyn: I love a new phone..But I am not that crazy..I have something to tell you..I don't want you to think I am crazy

Gary: I also have something to tell you

Marilyn: What is it?..Tell me

Gary: Come to my place..I will be there in ten minutes..You haven't been over in a while

Marilyn: You don't want me there..You always say that I am changing the look of your place

Gary: Babe..I don't want you to come and redecorate my place..You always do that..Just come and chill..I will buy you something to eat..What do you want to eat?

Marilyn: I don't have much appetite..You get something for yourself and I will get a bite..You don't have to get me anything

Gary: I will get you a fruit juice..Do you want a juice?

Marilyn: From where?

Gary: From the smoothie king

Marilyn: Ok..That will work

Gary: I will see you at my place in ten minutes babe

Marilyn: I don't want to get there before you

Gary: You have the key..Just get in

Marilyn: The key for your place?..I am not sure where I put it..Call me when you get home

Gary: Ok..No problem

_Gary's mom calls him on the phone..She has not seen him in a couple weeks..Usually Gary will stop by to talk and play with his siblings..His mom calls..Let's listen:

Gary: Hello

Gary's mom: Gary

Gary: Mom?

Gary's mom: Yes..You forgot?..I am still your mom..Where have you been?..I saw you two weeks ago..What is going on?

Gary: Well..Mom..I am sorry..I am not allowed to come home

Gary's mom: What do you mean?

Gary: Just that mom..Dad told me that I am allowed to come to his house

Gary's mom: What?..Your dad?..My husband? Gary senior?

Gary: Yes mom..Dad told me that I can't come back home

Gary's mom: Why?..What is happening..He can't do that..This is my home as well..He can't prevent you from seeing your brother and sister..He can't prevent you from visiting me..I think He lost his mind

Gary: Mom..It is what it is..We talk about it like men..He said I should not come around

Gary's mom: What is the reason behind this?

Gary: It is about Marilyn

Gary's mom: It is about Marilyn..The girl you are dating?

Gary: Yes

Gary's mom: Why your dad is so upset about Marilyn..What is going on?

Gary: Mom..It's a long story

Gary's mom: I don't care how long the story is..I need to hear it..Because..Your dad does not want my son to come home to see me..To see your siblings..I want to know about it now..I don't even care about what it is really about..I am already furious about it..I can't wait to see him..Anyway..What is it about?

Gary: Mom..Marilyn was infected with the HIV virus at her job..My dad wants me to break up with her and cut all ties with her because of that..I made him understand that this is not something I can do..He said to me..I don't want you to come around and put my family in danger

Gary's mom: Did he say that?

Gary: Yes..He did

Gary's mom: That does not sound like the man I am married..How could he make such an ignorant statement..I am sorry to hear about Marilyn situation..How is she doing?

Gary: She is ok

Gary's mom: As long you that you take certain precaution to not get infected..It's fine..There is no reason for you to stop coming home..I think your dad is the one who should move out..I want to see you today..This afternoon

Gary: Mom..I don't want to create any problem within the family

Gary's mom: There will be a big problem within the family if my son can't come to my house..And I mean it..Your dad must have been playing..Not in my house..I can't do that..I respect him..He is my husband for many years..But I am not going to tolerate such ignorance..Tonight you come to the house..I want to sit with you and your dad to go over this matter

Gary: Mom..It's not that serious..I am not a child anymore..I don't need to be around dad all the time

Gary's mom: It is serious Gary..It is not about your dad..Forget your dad..I want you to come home today

Gary: I will see mom

Gary's mom: Don't tell me I will see..Gary..You know better..You are getting me upset now

Gary: Ok..Ok mom..I will be there

Gary's mom: Ok..I will see you later

Gary: Ok mom..See you later

_A couple of weeks later..Gary goes to the clinic for the result of his test

Gary: Good morning

Nurse: Good morning..Are you today young man?

Gary: I am fine..I will be better if only I could be positive..She is running out of medications..I desperately need to be positive

Nurse: How much she has left?

Gary: Actually..She only has enough for tomorrow..After tomorrow..I don't know what she is going to do..That's her on the phone

Nurse: Answer it

Gary: Hello

Marilyn: Hello..Gary

Gary: Yes babe

Marilyn: I just realized t I don't have medication for today

Gary: Really?

Marilyn: I only have a couple of pills..But without all of them the cocktail is useless

Gary: I am sorry to hear that..We will find a way

Marilyn: I don't know what we are going to do Gary?..Remember the doctor said..One of not taking the medications could be very bad..The virus will unleash an aggressive attack against my white blood cells

Gary: Everything is going to be ok

Marilyn: Where are you Gary?..Can you stop by later..I am really scared

Gary: Definitely..I will see you later..Bye babe

Nurse: Ok..I have your envelop right here

Gary: Thank you

Nurse: You are welcome

Gary: Thank you god..Thank you god..Thank you..Oh..Thank you..Yes..Yes..I am positive

Nurse: You are crying..You will make me cry

Gary: I am positive..Those are tears of joy..She ran out of medications..Thank god..I am going to the hospital right now to get a prescription fill out

Nurse: You are such a brave young man..It is unbelievable

Gary: I have to run to the hospital

Nurse: The doctor can write you a prescription

Gary: The doctor..You mean here?

Nurse: Yes..Do you have your insurance card with you?

Gary: Yes I do

Nurse: Hold on..Let me go talk to him

Gary: Thank you

Nurse: Doctor Sanders..We have a young man here..He is HIV positive..He would like to know whether you can feel a prescription for his medications.

Dr. Sanders: He has to go to the first doctor who previously filled out the prescription

Nurse: He does not have one..He just found out that he is positive and he wants to start taking his drugs right away

Dr. Sanders: Does he have health insurance?

Nurse: Yes he does

Dr. Sanders: Send him in..I will interview him first then I will write the prescription..Let him fill out the forms

Nurse: Thank you Doctor

Dr. Sanders: No problem

Gary: What did he say?

Dr. Sanders: He said ok..He wants to talk to you first

Gary: Can I go in now?

Nurse: Yes you can..Fill out these forms

Gary: Thank you

Nurse: You are welcome

_A few minutes later

Gary: I am done with the form

Nurse: Thank you..You need to sign right here as well

Gary: Thank you

Nurse: Do you have your insurance card?

Gary: Yes I do

Nurse: I need to make copy of it

Gary: Sure..Here it is..Should I tell him that I got myself contaminated on purpose?

Nurse: No..I would not tell that..He is very serious..You never know how he would react to it..He might choose not to be part of that

Gary: What should I say?

Nurse: You are asking the wrong person..I never got myself contaminated with a deadly disease on purpose..It is all up to you

Gary: I know what I would say..I will say that I got infected at my job

Nurse: Here's your card

Gary: I feel a little fever

Nurse: It's all in your mind..I don't think you will start having fever yet..The positive result is because has started to create anti HIV cells..But I don't think you will have fever yet..Anyway..The doctor is waiting for you..Good luck

Gary: Thank you

Nurse: Dr. Sanders..You want me to send the young man in?

Dr. Sanders: Send him in

Nurse: The doctor is waiting to see you

Gary: Thank you

Dr. Sanders: Come in

Gary: Good morning Doctor

Dr. Sanders: Good morning..Have a sit please

Gary: Thank you

Dr. Sanders: Let me close the door..Do you want something to drink

Gary: Water..Do you have water?

Dr. Sanders: Yes..In large quantity..I am a fan of water..I don't drink soda..Not even juice

Gary: That's very healthy

Dr. Sanders: The nurse told me that you are HIV positive..Is that right?

Gary: Yes sir..I am positive

Dr. Sanders: You know this could just be a false positive..If you want I can schedule another test for you

Gary: That won't be necessary..I believe that I am positive..I am ready to rock and roll

Dr. Sanders: You seem to be very upbeat about it..Do you know that you can from it..To this day..There is no cure for it..Thank god for you have a good insurance plan..Otherwise you could have died

Gary: I understand..This is why I want to be aggressive against the disease..I want to go get my medications right away..Can you do that for me..Can you write me a prescription?

Dr. Sanders: Yes..I am a general and you had the test done here at my clinic..I should be able to write you a prescription

Gary: Thank you..I really appreciate it

Dr. Sanders: I like your attitude towards this..This is the kind of attitude one should have to fight that virus..You are almost happy about it..If I did not know better that's what I would say

Gary: Well..I am happy that I can afford to buy the medications..Some people cannot do so..They are in a more difficult situation

Dr. Sanders: You are absolutely correct..Being able to get the medications give a chance to fight

Gary: Having a chance to fight is something everybody deserves..This is why I am happy right now doctor

Dr. Sanders: I may say this..During my twenty something years in practice..You are the bravest patient I have met

Gary: Thank you

Dr. Sanders: Here's your prescription for the drugs cocktail..I put seven refills in it for you..I would like to see you in a week..To see the effect of the medications..Draw some blood..Make the appointment at the front desk..There is a co payment..I believe it's ten dollars..If you don't have it with you..You can bring it next time..The nurse will write the appointments for you

Gary: Thank you so much

Dr. Sanders: I will see you in a couple of weeks

Gary: Ok

Nurse: Everything worked out ok

Gary: Yes..Everything is fine

Nurse: Dr. Sanders is a sweetheart

Gary: He is the nicest guy..He wrote the prescription for me

Nurse: Now..The mission has begun?

Gary: Yes..I am honored to have the opportunity to save someone's life..Even when I have to put my life in jeopardy..It is worthwhile

Nurse: Good luck to you..I will pray for you..So god can keep you..And you never get sick

Gary: Thank you

Nurse: Don't forget..Keep me posted..If you need anything let me know

Gary: Thank you

_Following those words Gary runs out of the doctor's office as it was on fire..Gets in his car and left tire marks on the ground..He drives straight to the pharmacy..I don't think a NASCAR driver would have been able to keep up with him..He arrives at the pharmacy and rushes towards the pharmacist..Let's listen:

Gary: Good morning..Sir..Sir..I have an emergency..Sir..Can you help me please

Pharmacist: Did you say you have an emergency?

Gary: Yes sir

Pharmacist: You know this is not a hospital..Right?

Gary: Yes sir..I know that

Pharmacist: Is this a medication for a cardiac patient?

Gary: No..It's for me sir

Gary: Her it is

Pharmacist: I see..You know that disease does not kill you as quickly as a heart attack..Right?

Gary: I know that

Pharmacy: Why the urgency?

Gary: I just want to stay on top of it

Pharmacist: You know how to take the medications?

Gary: I know sir..The doctor went over that in detail with me

Pharmacist: You have six refills left

Gary: Thank you

_Gary rushes out of the pharmacy and into his car..He drives to Marilyn's home..In less than ten minutes he is there..Let's go in with him:

Mindy: Lyn..Someone is ringing the bell

Marilyn: Mom..I don't feel too well..Can you get it for me?

Mindy: Where are you?..What happened to you?..You have so many lumps on your arms..They are all over your body..What happened baby?

Marilyn: I don't mom..It must be an allergic reaction

Mindy: The person is breaking the bell..Yes..I am coming

Gary: Hello

Mindy: Gary..It is you..You need to use the bathroom

Gary: No

Mindy: What was the urgency Gary?..You almost gave me a heart attack

Gary: I am sorry..Where is Lyn?

Mindy: She is in her room..She is not feeling too well today

Gary: Lyn..Are you ok?

Marilyn: I am not..Look at my arms..Mom..Close the door please

Gary: What happened..It must be an allergic reaction

Marilyn: it is not Gary..I haven't taken the medications for two days now

Gary: I thought it was just one day?

Marilyn: I did not want you to worry..I am dying Gary

Gary: No..You are not dying babe..I am not going to let you die

Marilyn: Look at me..Just in a couple of days..What am I going to do?

Gary: Lyn..I have something for you

Marilyn: I am not in the mood for food Gary..You remember I told you that I will die..You were telling me no..No..We will find a way

Gary: Baby..You are not dying..I have it..Please..Stop crying..Open your eyes..Look

Marilyn: What..What is that?

Gary: Look

Marilyn: Those are the medications

Gary: Yes..I got them for you babe..You remember..I promised you..I am with you

Marilyn: Where did you find them Gary?

Gary: I did..I did

Marilyn: Did you rob the pharmacy?

Gary: Rob is an understatement..I emptied it

Marilyn: Gary?

Gary: I might as well put the pharmacy sign on my car's trunk

Marilyn: This is not funny Gary..If you robbed the pharmacy..I don't want them

Gary: C'mon babe..You know me better than that..We are not to that point yet

Marilyn: What do you mean yet?

Gary: Babe..Take the medications to get rid of the lumps

Marilyn: Where?

Gary: Where what?

Marilyn: Where did you find them?

Gary: Take them first then I will tell you..Let me get some water for you

Marilyn: I have water right here..Thank you so much..I was about to die..Thank you..What would I do without you?

Gary: What would I do without you..You give me the opportunity to love and share that abundant reservoir that god puts in everyone of us..Thank you for giving me a chance to use it..Also a chance to learn to trust

Marilyn: I can't even put into words what you have done for me since I met you..You are an angel that god sent from above..I don't know how I would be able to cope with my mother's cancer..And now this..I was just grieving my dad when my mother was diagnosed with cancer..Then I got infected with this disease..I don't know how I would have been able to do it without you..Even though your dad did not want you to stay with me..You did anyway..I really appreciate you Gary

Gary: Well does not understand..There is an author by the name of Phito Polycarpe who wrote:

"When someone is being battered by raging waves and is drowning

This is no time to teach the techniques and fundamentals of swimming

This is rather the time to gather the materials of love to build a raft and begin the process of rescuing"

Marilyn: Nice..Where did you read that Gary

Gary: Actually..That author Phito Polycarpe is one of my favorites..You have to check him out

Marilyn: I sure will

Gary: You took them all

Marilyn: I did..I started to feel better already..Now..Tell me where you found them

Gary: I will tell you later

Marilyn: Why not now?..Remember I told I had something to tell you

Gary: What is it?

Marilyn: I talked with my dad

Gary: What do you mean you talked to your dad?

Marilyn: My dad came to visit me

Gary: C'mon Lyn..Stop playing

Marilyn: I am not playing Gary..You know I don't play with stuffs like that..I would not joke using my dad's name

Gary: Where did you see him?

Marilyn: In my room..I was alone here..I heard the door opened when I look I saw my dad standing by my bed

Gary: Babe..It is because you are stressed out..It's your mind that is playing trick on you

Marilyn: Don't say that to me Gary..I thought you would be the only person who would believe me

Gary: I am sorry babe..I want to believe you but at the same time there is a part of me that prevents me from doing so

Marilyn: You always say that you trust me

Gary: I do babe..But this is much different..The supernatural does not exist..It is fabricated by the human's mind

Marilyn: My mom even smelled his cologne in my room..I thought she believed me..I heard her talking to her friend Beth and she told her..I think my daughter is losing her mind

Gary: It's going to be hard for anyone to believe something like that

Marilyn: Oh my god..I am not crazy..I did talk to my dad

Gary: There is no need to be upset about it..It's just impossible to talk to your dad..It is your mind that is playing trick on you

Marilyn's dad: Yes..She did talk to me

Marilyn: Dad?..Where are you?

Gary: Who's voice is that?

Marilyn: Dad?

Marilyn's dad: I am right here

Marilyn: Dad..You come through the wall..You scared me

Gary: Who is this?..How did you get here?

Marilyn: That's my dad Gary..Dad this is Gary

Marilyn's dad: Hello young man..She told me about you the other day

Marilyn: See..I told you that my dad visited me before..You did not believe me

Gary: I am in shock..I am afraid

Marilyn's dad: No need to be afraid..We don't hurt people..I am only here to comfort Lyn

Gary: Yes sir

Marilyn's dad: I really appreciate the help and support you had given her.,Just don't rob the pharmacy

Marilyn: Dad..How do you know about the pharmacy?

Gary: You heard what I said about robbing the pharmacy?

Marilyn's dad: I did

Gary: It was only a joke

Marilyn's dad: I know..You are a good kid

Marilyn: Dad..Thank you for stopping by..Gary did not believe me

Gary: I am sorry..I am believer now

Marilyn's dad: I have to leave now

Marilyn: Thank you dad

Marilyn's dad: Stay together..I will send help for you ok

Marilyn: What kind of help?..Dad..Dad?

Gary: He left through the wall

Marilyn: Dad..Are you still there?

Gary: He is gone Lyn

Marilyn: Oh my god..Oh my god..Mom..Mom..Mom

Mindy: Lyn..You are going to give me a heart attack..What is it?

Marilyn: Dad was here

Mindy: C'mon Lyn..I don't have time to play

Marilyn: Mom..Dad was here

Mindy: I know..You told me that last week..Everybody thinks you are losing your mind..You need to stop that

Marilyn: Mom..He was here just now

Mindy: Well..You should have introduced Gary to him..You should go see a doctor about that

Gary: She did

Mindy: What did you say?

Gary: She did introduce me to her dad

Mindy: Wait a minute..Is this some type of joke guys?

Marilyn: He was here..You have to believe me

Gary: He was here

Mindy: I am done with that kind of thought..Lyn is losing her mind..Now you too Gary

Marilyn's dad: No..They are not

Marilyn: Dad?..Is that you?..Are you coming back?..Please come back..Mom is here..Please

Marilyn's dad: Hi..I see her..Dad..I was expecting you from that wall

Mindy: Oh my god..Oh my god..Oh my god

Marilyn's dad: Let her sit down..Sit down..It's me..I come to visit my daughter

Mindy: I see that..I see that..How are you?..Oh god..I miss you so much

Marilyn's dad: I miss you guys too

Mindy: Can I give you a hug?

Marilyn's dad: No..You can't

Marilyn: You can't mom

Marilyn's Dad: I have to go..I already stayed out too long

Mindy: We have been through so much since you've been gone

Marilyn's Dad: I know..I am sorry..You will be fine..The cancer will go on remission and Lyn will be fine too

Mindy: Thank you

Marilyn's dad: I can't stay any longer

Mindy: Bye honey

Marilyn: Bye dad

Marilyn's dad: Bye guys..Take care

Gary: How did he go through the wall?

Marilyn: I have no idea

Mindy: Who's medication are those on night stand

Marilyn: Mine mom..You are too nosey mom..Gary brought me some medicines for the allergy

Mindy: That's nice..You look better already..They are almost gone..You are not a doctor yet Gary..You should not prescribe medications

Gary: I know..I know that..Soon

_A couple of weeks later

Thomas: Are you positive yet?

Gary: Yes I am

Thomas: Really?..You don't look sick at all

Gary: Yes..You did not even know anything..This is to show you there is no need to discriminate against those who are infected with that virus..My phone is ringing..Hold on

Marilyn: Hello

Gary: Hello Lyn

Marilyn: Hello Gary

Gary: You need me babe

Marilyn: Yes..Can you stop by please

Gary: Right now?

Marilyn: Right now

Gary: What is it babe?..Tell me

Marilyn: I can't talk to you about it on the phone

Gary: Ok..I am on my way

Thomas: What is it?

Gary: She said she needs to talk to me

Thomas: Ok..I will talk to you later

_A few minutes later..Gary was at Marilyn's home..Let's listen:

Marilyn: You are here already?..You drive too fast Gary

Gary: Not really..What is it you want to talk about?

Marilyn: Gary..I think I am pregnant

Marilyn: I have morning sickness..I am having

Gary: Really?.Why would you think that?

Marilyn: I am having craving for strange food..I really think that I am..But..How could it be Gary..You used protection every time..Right?

Gary: I need to tell you the truth Marilyn..I did not use protection every time..This is why you might be pregnant

Marilyn: Why would you do such a thing? Are you crazy?..You know I am infected..You should go and have some test done

Gary: I did already

Marilyn: Are you ok?

Gary: I am ok..You meant whether I am positive or not?

Marilyn: Yes..You are negative right?

Gary: No

Marilyn: What do you mean no Gary?

Gary: I am positive Lyn

Marilyn: No..Don't tell me that Gary..I don't want you to die

Gary: Don't cry..I am not going to die

Marilyn: Oh..What have I done?

Gary: You are fine babe..You did not do anything wrong..Don't cry

Marilyn: The guilt of seeing you getting sick will kill me way before that disease

Gary: You did not do anything..I did it on purpose..I removed the protection every time during sex

Marilyn: I am so angry with you now..Now both of us are sick..Why..Why Gary?

Gary: I wanted to save your life..This is how I was able to get the medications for you..I bought them with my insurance card

Marilyn: Gary..You got infected so you could buy medications ad share them with me?

Gary: I had no choice Lyn

Marilyn: Yes..You had a choice..You stay away and not get contaminated

Gary: That's the only choice I had..I promised you that I would do everything I could to help you

Marilyn: When your dad finds out..What's going to happen?

Gary: He will not find out

Marilyn: What are we going to do with the baby?

Gary: We are going to keep it..I am against abortion

Marilyn: Me too..But the baby will be born with the virus

Gary: Not necessarily..A large percentage of babies from mothers who have HIV are not born with the virus

Marilyn: Really?

Gary: Yes..It is the truth..So I think we should take the chance

Marilyn: If we die..The bay will be able to carry on with our lives..Who will take care of the baby?

Gary: My mom would be happy to do so..Let's hope the baby is healthy..That could be a blessing

_A couple months into the pregnancy..Gary and Marilyn run into some serious obstacles..According to the law of the state..It is required for a pregnancy to be terminated if the mother is HIV positive..Gary and Marilyn have no intention of terminate the pregnancy..They both want to keep the baby..After all they both think if they leave the planet..The baby would be able continue living for them..Having an abortion would very difficult for Marilyn to accept..Gary and Marilyn are at the clinic..Let's listen:

Nurse: Ma'am..We have a little problem

Marilyn: What is it please?..We are paying cash for the check up

Nurse: No it does not have anything to do with payment

Gary: What is it?

Nurse: According to the law of the state..It is illegal for a mother who is HIV positive to keep a baby

Marilyn: Excuse me?

Nurse: Mom..This is the law of the state

Gary: It does not make any sense..Most kids born with mothers that are HIV positive are not infected..Therefore..I don't understand it

Nurse: I am just telling you..They are very strict about that..People got arrested before for not obeying the law

Gary: This is pure nonsense

Marilyn: I am not going to kill my baby because of some men who have never gotten pregnant..What kind of law is this

Nurse: Don't get mad at me..I am just telling you guys what the law is..We have to inform you

Gary: How would they find out anyway?

Nurse: Our office has to report it to the state within twenty four hours

Gary: You guys do the snitching

Nurse: Well sir..We are required to inform the state

_Gary and Marilyn left the clinic that day a bit disappointed regarding the news..But..They were not phase to the fact that they will not kill their baby because of some law put in place by some men sitting behind their desks in Washington..A couple of weeks later..Marilyn received a call..Let's listen:

Marilyn: Hello

State Employee: Hello..Good morning

Marilyn: Good morning

State Employee: I would like to speak with Marilyn

Marilyn: This is Marilyn..How can I help you..Are you the lady who called the other day trying to sell life insurance?

State Employee: No ma'am..This call is about life but not life insurance

Marilyn: How can I help you?

State Employee: Ma'am base on your medical record..You have to terminate your pregnancy as soon as possible

Marilyn: Excuse me?..I don't understand you

State Employee: Try your best to understand ma'am..This is a very important matter

Marilyn: No..It will not happen..This is my body..No one is going to tell me what to do with it

State Employee: Ma'am..My call today is to inform you about the law

Marilyn: Forget your law..And get off my phone

State Employee: You will be criminally charged if you don't comply

Marilyn: Good bye

_Following the conversation with the State employee..Marilyn called Gary on the phone..Let's listen:

Gary: Hello

Marilyn: I can't believe this

Gary: You can't believe what?..Calm down babe..I don't understand a word you are saying

Marilyn: The state called me and told me to basically kill my baby

Gary: They called?

Marilyn: Yes they did..She told me it has to done as soon as possible

Gary: They must be crazy..We need this little baby..That's our only chance of living a long life

Marilyn: They must be crazy..She told me..If I don't comply criminal charges will be brought against me

_A couple of weeks later..Marilyn is at Gary's apartment when his doorbell rings..Who could it be?

Gary: Babe..Go see who is at the door for me

Marilyn: Ok..It must be your friend Thomas..Watch him leaves as he sees me here

Detective: Good morning

Marilyn: Good morning

Detective: Are you Marilyn?

Marilyn: Yes

Detective: I am detective Johnson..You are under arrest ma'am

Marilyn: Under arrest for what?

Detective: For failure to comply with the law of the state

Marilyn: Don't touch me..Babe..Come here

Gary: what is going on..Hey..Hey.. Get your hands off her

Detective: Stand back sir..I am detective Roberts..We are here to make an arrest..You need to stand clear and let my partner handcuff the lady..Or you will be charge for interference

Gary: This is my girlfriend..What did she do?

Detective: You can ask the judge that question..We are executing a warrant issued by the state court

Gary: This is nonsense..This is so unfair..She is pregnant..Be careful..Don't push her

Detective: Sir..You are making things worse..Nobody is pushing her..She is resisting..Stop resisting ma'am..You can be charged for that too..Just go see the judge and you will come back home

Gary: Do you really have to put the handcuff on her

Detective: The handcuff is to protect us and to protect her..No need to get upset..You will go see the judge and you will come back home..If you have a lawyer sir..Contact your lawyer

Gary: Where are you taking her?

Detective: Downtown

Marilyn: Babe..Look in my phone you will find a number..The firm is called Marlon & Marvin Firm..Call them please

Detective: No need to cry and get upset..Get her some water

Marilyn: They are trying to kill my baby..They want to kill my baby

Detective: Nobody is trying to kill your baby..You are going to get sick and end up in the hospital..Just calm down..Give her the water..Open your mouth..Drink some

Marilyn: Leave me alone

Detective: I am going to put the handcuffs with your arms in front..You can be more comfortable..Ok sir..She will be downtown..You can come there and work out a bail deal for her..She should be able to see a judge regarding her bail today

Gary: Don't worry babe..I will be there

Marilyn: Call the lawyers

Gary: Don't worry babe

_Following those words..Marilyn is put in the back of the detectives' car and they sped away..Gary's head was spinning..It is about as much she can handle right now..He is not feeling too well..He feels a little chill throughout his body..A sign that he might have a fever..But he has no time to think about himself..Marilyn is in a worse situation and Gary has to act quickly..He does not know where to start..Should he call the lawyers..Should he go to the police station..Should he take some medications..He does not know where to start..He decides to call the lawyers..Let's listen:

Secretary: Hello

Gary: Hello..May I speak with Marlon please?

Secretary: Marlon is not in at this time

Gary: Can I speak with one of the lawyers?

Secretary: Yes..Hold on please

Chris: Hello

Secretary: Chris..I have someone on line one who wants to speak with one of you guys

Chris: That's the same guy from last week?

Secretary: No..I don't think so

Chris: Send the call in

Secretary: Ok

Chris: Hello..This is Chris..How can I help you?

Gary: Hello Chris..My name is Gary..I am calling on behalf of my fiancée..She got arrested

Chris: What she got arrested for?

Gary: For being pregnant

Chris: Did you say for being pregnant?

Gary: Yes sir

Chris: What country you are calling form..We don't handle litigation overseas..We only work in the United States..What country are you calling from?

Gary: I am in the United States sir

Chris: You mean the land of the free and the home of the braves?

Gary: Yes sir

Chris: Didn't you say she got arrested for being pregnant?

Gary: Yes sir

Chris: Last time I checked being pregnant was not a crime

Gary: Well..She is HIV positive..They say she should terminate her pregnancy as soon as possible..She did not do it fast enough..They put her in jail

Chris: And all this is happening in the United States?

Gary: Yes sir

Marvin: What's going on?

Marlon: Hey Chris

Chris: Hold on just one second please..My partners just walked in my office here

Gary: No problem

Marvin: What is it about? I heard you mentioned..Is this happening in the United States

Marlon: What is going on?

Chris: A lady got arrested because she is pregnant

Marlon: Why?

Chris: Because she is HIV positive

Marlon: Some states where abortions are illegal give the woman free will to end the pregnancy..I never heard someone put in jail for refusal to end a pregnancy

Marvin: Things are changing every day..It is time for actions

Marlon: Who is on the phone?

Chris: Her fiancé

Marlon: Put him on speaker

Chris: Hello..Can you hear me Gary?

Gary: Yes I can

Chris: My partners Marvin and Marlon would like to speak with you as well

Gary: Hello guys

Marlon: Gary..How long since she's been in jail?

Gary: Not too long ago

Marlon: You would like us to represent her..Right?

Gary: Yes..Please

Marlon: What do you say guys..We are going to handle it?

Marvin: I don't see why not

Marlon: What do you say Chris?

Chris: Definitely

Marlon: Ok Gary..We are all on board..We are riding with you..Can you stop by sometimes today or tomorrow to fill out some papers..I will say today is better..So we can get the ball rolling..And try to get her out on bail

Gary: No problem..I will stop by..You guys are located at Franklin Street

Marvin: We are no longer at Franklin Street..That's the old address..We are on Main Street..The beige building at the corner of Steward Ave and Main Street

Gary: Ok..I will be there

Marlon: See you soon

_Gary then calls his mom on the phone ..Let's listen:

Gary's mom: Hello

Gary: Mom..Mom

Gary's mom: Yes Gary..I am listening..What is it?

Gary: Mom..I need your help

Gary's mom: What is it Gary?

Gary: Mom..I need your help

Gary's mom: Gary I am listening

Gary: Mom..Marilyn is in jail

Gary's mom: In jail?..For what?

Gary: She got arrested for being pregnant

Gary's mom: What do you mean for being pregnant?..Is she?

Gary: Yes she is mom

Gary's mom: Gary..How did that happen?

Gary: I don't know mom

Gary's mom: Gary..Are you not using protection?

Gary: Mom..One of them might have had a hole in it

Gary's mom: Gary..This is very serious..How can I help you?..How she got arrested for being pregnant

Gary: Mom..The state wanted her to terminate the pregnancy and she refused

Gary's mom: What her pregnancy has to do with the government?

Gary: Some states required that you end the pregnancy if the carrier is HIV positive

Gary's mom: That's news to me

Gary: You wouldn't know mom..It does not happen that often..Mom..I need you to help me with the lawyers' fee

Gary's mom: Have you found a lawyer yet?

Gary: Yes mom..I need you to help me

Gary's mom: How much is it going to be to represent her?

Gary: They did not tell me yet

Gary's mom: I will put some money on your account tomorrow

Gary: Ok mom..Thank you

Gary's mom: Ten thousands should be enough

Gary: I am not sure mom

Gary's mom: If she is going to trial..Ten thousand will not be enough..I will put fifty thousands in there for you just to start..Let me know how much it is going to be

Gary: Thanks mom..Somebody on the other line

Gary's mom: Talk to you later

Gary: Ok mom..Thanks..Hello

Mindy: Hello..Gary?

Gary: Hello Mindy..How are you?

Mindy: Have you heard from Marilyn..She told me she would be with you..I called her phone..She did not answer

Gary: Uh..There was a little incident

Mindy: What kind of incident..Is she ok?

Gary: She is fine..I will have her call you soon

Mindy: What happened to her?

Gary: I will have her call you

Mindy: Is she at the hospital

Gary: Yes..She has a stomach pain..I had to take her to the hospital

Mindy: She might be having a miscarriage

Gary: I will tell her to call you as soon as she is able to

Mindy: Thank you Gary..Call me

_At the Law firm

Chris: You know who called me yesterday

Marvin: Who?

Chris: Khloe

Marvin: The prosecutor?

Chris: She is no longer a prosecutor..She quit the job at the D.A office..She wants to do criminal defense work now

Marvin: Really?..I think she will do well as a defense attorney..She is such a fighter

Chris: I know..I heard that she and Kourt were a problem during the "Good Deed" trial

Marvin: It was like the UFC in there

Chris: Marlon..What do you think?..Should I invite her into this case?

Marlon: Which case?

Chris: The induced delivery case

Marlon: Well..I think we should start it to see where it is going..Then we can bring her in

Marvin: I agree..Remember she has not yet done any work as a defense lawyer

Marlon: I am not too concerned about that..She is a very talented attorney..The switch from prosecutor to defense should not be a problem

Chris: You are absolutely right..We all work for the D.A. at one point

Marvin: Not me

Marlon: I did work for the D.A..For just one case..I wanted to stand against my brother when he chose to defend that guy who sent him to jail for many years..And caused so much pain to my family

Chris: What case was that?.."The Family" case?

Marvin: Yes.."The Family"..That maniac came after me with all his might..It was fun though

Marlon: That was the worst decision you have made in your entire life

Marvin: What decision are you talking about?

Marlon: To represent that guy in court

Marvin: C'mon Marlon..I had no choice..The guy called me and asked me to represent him

Chris: That was the guy who committed the crime that caused you to spend many years in prison

Marlon: I know..Right..Dad died because of that

Marvin: C'mon guys..Enough already..Are we going to go back to the "Family" case..Or we are going to move on and embrace the "I am with you" case

Chris: We are ready..But it important that we remind you of it every so often

Marlon: You guys can try contacting Khloe..I will try to go to the jail and meet with the client and see how she is doing

Marvin: No problem..You what is going to happen..Kourt will want to be in the case as well

Chris: They know each other?

Marvin: Of course..They were in the "Good Deed" case together

Chris: As prosecutor and defense lawyer

Marvin: They became best friend

Marlon: Marvin..You take care of the ladies..You call Khloe and Kourt..You are the ladies' man

Marvin: I am?..I thought Chris was

Chris: You are Marv..You have the trophy this year

Marvin: Whatever guys

Marlon: Chris you want to go with me?

Chris: Where?

Marlon: To the jail..I want to see how the client is doing

Chris: No problem

Marvin: The client's fiancé is on his way here..Right?

Marlon: His name is Gary..Right Chris?

Chris: Yes

_Meanwhile..Gary's phone is ringing..Let's listen:

Gary: Hello..Kim

Kim: Hello..How are you Gary?

Gary: Not too good

Kim: What happened?..Marilyn is in the hospital?

Gary: No..Not the hospital

Kim: I've been calling her and she is not answering her phone..I called her mom she said..She thinks something happened..She is in the hospital

Gary: Yes..I let her believe she is in the hospital..I did not want to tell her that she is in jail

Kim: In jail?..Did you say in jail?

Gary: Yes she got arrested

Kim: For what..Got arrested for what?

Gary: Basically..For refusing to end her pregnancy

Kim: They cannot arrest her because of that

Gary: Well..That's what I thought

Kim: Where is she now?

Gary: She is at the jail

Kim: Have you found her a lawyer yet?

Gary: I have a meeting this afternoon at a firm

Kim: I know a couple of guys..They are very good

Gary: Who are they?

Kim: The guys at the MCM Firm..Marlon..Marlon Chris Marvin Law firm

Gary: That's where I am going this afternoon

Kim: They are really good..They are my friends..Can I go to the jail and see her?

Gary: You can try to

Kim: I am heading there..I had to leave this afternoon for Spain..I am going to cancel that business trip..I have to be there for her

Gary: Thank you Kim..I will talk to you later

Kim: Tell the guys that you know me..Tell them Marilyn is my best friend

Gary: Will do

Meanwhile..Marlon and Chris are at the jail to visit Marilyn

C.O.: Form one line please..One line please..Car keys and phone in the basket please

Marlon: Good afternoon

C.O.: Good afternoon counselor..Long time no see counselor

Marlon: I know..I know

C.O.: Good afternoon Mr. Chris

Chris: Good afternoon

C.O.: Where have you guys been?

Chris: You are talking as if we escaped from your jail

Marlon: I know..Right

C.O.: It feels like it

Marlon: You are right about that..We used to be here so often..Sometimes..Three times a day

C.O.: I made a request for a cell for y'all

Chris: Thanks..But no thanks..Your hotel is not equipped enough

C.O.: We can add the ladies to the list for you

Marlon: Don't make empty promises..Chris is very serious when it comes to the ladies

Chris: You might find me in one of your cells waiting

C.O.: Very funny..Who you guys are here to see today?

Marlon: Marilyn April

C.O.: You don't usually have female clients

Marlon: What can I do..With this guy Chris in the office..They don't stop calling

Chris: The honeys comes to the bear

C.O.: I thought it was the bear that goes to the honey?

Marlon: Not in this case..Chris is different

C.O.: The female inmates are held on the left side..Go through that gate..The building is on the right..Give the paper to the C.O. and they will bring her to you guys..Nice to see you guys

Chris: We are not here to see you..I am here on a date with the inmate

C.O.: I believe you..Let me know if you need a room

Chris: Sure..She has a room already..Doesn't she?

C.O.: She has a cellmate..Y'all can have a double date

Marlon: I will pass on that..Thank you anyway C.O.,Just go straight..Right?

C.O.: Yes..You are welcome

Meanwhile..Gary arrives at the law office to meet Marvin

Gary: Good afternoon

Secretary: Good afternoon..How can I help you?

Gary: I am here to see a lawyer..I talked to them on the phone..They are expecting me

Secretary: One minute please..Hello

Marvin: Yes..What is it again..Are you going to let me do some work today?

Secretary: Yes..Your work is here..Gary is here

Marvin: Send him in

Secretary: You can go in..He is waiting for you

Marvin: Hello..Hello..Have a seat please

Gary: Thank you..Thank you

Marvin: As you can see..I am alone here..Marlon and Chris went to the jail to meet Marilyn

Gary: Really?..That's nice..I would not think they would do such thing in such a hurry

Marvin: We take our job very serious..Our client is everything..Especially that case..It does not have any precedent..Therefore..Creating a precedent that will challenge the unfair law is very important

Gary: I did not know they would go as far as putting her in prison

Marvin: Well..This is an opportunity to make an example out of her..This is why we have to go strong

Gary: How much will it cost?

Marvin: As you may know..We are the best out there..We charge our clients but they get their money worth..We are not cheap

Gary: Can you give me an idea of how much it would be

Marvin: It all depends on how much work is required and the duration of the trial..We can also work out a flat rate for you

Gary: Marilyn is also best friend with Kim

Marvin: Kim..She knows Kim?

Gary: They are actually best friend..She is on her way to the jail right now to go see Marilyn

Marvin: I see..She is a sweetheart

Gary: How you guys get to know her

Marvin: We know her for years..She works in the fashion industry..Chris is the one who introduced Kim to us..They dated for a while..She was too serious for Chris..He is a player..He has no intention in setting down..So..Kim moved on..She remains good friend to us

Gary: Marilyn and her are best buddies..Since Marilyn knows Kim..Can you guys work out a family rate for us?

Marvin: Definitely..I will tell you what I am going to do..I know the guys are going to kill me for this..We usually require that a client put down a down payment of one hundred thousand..In an account so we can take care of the expenses..Then at the end of the trial the client is billed

Gary: Ok..You guys are pretty expensive..Well..We do a great job..Protecting one's freedom is priceless

Gary: I understand

Marvin: Because you are family..You know Kim..Our client is best friend with her..I will do it for you for eighty..The deposit is going to be only eighty instead of one hundred

Gary: What about seventy five

Marvin: You are twisting my arm here young man..Well..I will do it for you for seventy five..I know my guys are going to kill me..Seventy five deposit

Gary: Let me call my mom and tell her about it..She is the one paying for it..Of course I will have to pay her when I graduate

Marvin: What is your major Gary?

Gary: I am in medical school

Marvin: You will be fine..Those guys make the big bucks..You can use our phone here if you want to

Gary: I will use my cell..Mom

Gary's mom: Hi..Have you heard any news of Marilyn?

Gary: I am at the law firm..Two of the lawyers went to meet with her

Gary's mom: That's nice..That's a bad situation to be in..She is pregnant..Did you ask them how much it will cost?

Gary: I did mom..It's going to be a seventy five thousand dollars deposit..Then after the trial they bill the client

Gary's mom: Seventy five uh?..Gary..When are you going to pay me back?

Gary: Don't worry mom..I will pay you back

Gary's mom: I will put the money in your account tomorrow

Gary: No mom put it in the firm's account

Gary's mom: Get the information from them and I will do so tomorrow

Gary: Thank you mom

Gary's mom: You are welcome...Are you going to visit her?

Gary: as soon as I leave here I will go

Gary's mom: Give her my regards ok..Tell her to be strong..I have to go baby..I am waiting for a very important call

Gary: What call mom

Gary's mom: Gary..You are not my husband..Even your dad doesn't ask me such question..A business call..Are you satisfied now?

Gary: I will talk to you later mom..Thank you

Gary's mom: You are welcome my love..Call me and let me know

Gary: Ok

Marvin: what did mom say? She agrees to pay it

Gary: Yes

Marvin: It's good to have a mom with deep pocket

Gary: Mom is alright..Dad is ok too..But my mom has more money

Marvin: What does she do?

Gary: Mom is a business lady..She has two hotels..She has a partner but she has a larger share..And she has four franchises

Marvin: Restaurants?

Gary: Yes..She is ok

Marvin: I see..She is more than ok

Gary: I need the information regarding the account in which to make the deposit

Marvin: Our secretary will take care of that..She will give you all the info

Secretary: Hello

Khlo: May I speak with Chris please?

Secretary: Chris is not in at this time

Khlo: May I speak with Marlon?

Secretary: He is not in either..Do you want to speak with Marvin?

Khlo: Marvin is there?..Sure..Let me talk to him

Secretary: Hold on please..Marvin..Someone on the line for you

Marvin: Send the call in..Hello

Khlo: Hey handsome..I want to speak to your brother

Marvin: Khlo..How are you love..Where have you been?..Talk to me..My brother is me

Khlo: I heard about that case..I want to be in

Marvin: Really?..Are you sure?..It's going to be bloody

Khlo: C'mon..You know me better

Marvin: How is Kourt doing?

Khlo: She is fine..I was with her last night..She is probably sleeping..She can't drink and she had a cocktail last night

Marvin: I see

Khlo: Where are the guys?

Marvin: Your boyfriend Chris?

Khlo: My boyfriend?..My days of being with a womanizer are gone..I am no longer trying to fit in

Marvin: I hear you

Khlo: I think Chris does not want to grow up..He certainly enjoys the attention from the all women at all times..I think it's childish..And I have already turned that page

Marvin: Who is the man now?

Khlo: For me to know and for you to find out..Mister Marvin..Questioning me like I am on the stand

Marvin: Ok..Ok..I am sorry

Khlo: You know Kourt will want to be in once she finds out that I am in the case

Marvin: I think the best thing to do is to bring at least three women due to the nature of the case

Khlo: Who else do you have in mind?

Marvin: I want to bring Renee in..She is a very smart young lawyer..Initially..She studied business law..Then she transition to criminal

Khlo: Just like me

Marvin: I did not know you were a business lawyer

Khlo: Of course baby..Where have you been?..I did business law then three years later I moved into criminal

Marvin: You were asking me for the guys

Khlo: Yes..Until you turned the conversation about Chris

Marvin: I know..The guys went to see the client..She is pregnant and also her health condition..They went to make sure she is provided with all that she needs to prevent her health from deteriorating

Khlo: I see..You guys are the best

Marvin: The guys are going to be in the room but we will let the ladies take charge of the case..I think it's a good time to bring in Malika

Khlo: That would be great..Four ladies..It would be great

Marvin: We will see..I have to meet with the guys regarding this first

Khlo: Just let me know..Say hello to Marlon for me

Marvin: And Chris

Khlo: Of course..And Chris

Marvin: Next week we will have a meeting with everyone..So we can go over which role each one of us is going to play

Meanwhile..Marlon and Chris are at the detention center to meet with Marilyn

C.O.: Table number ten please

Marilyn: Which one?

C.O.: Number ten

Marilyn: Thank you

Marlon: Hello

Marilyn: Hello

Chris: Have a seat please..I am Chris

Marlon: I am Marlon

Marilyn: You guys are the lawyers

Marlon: Yes we are

Chris: We are here to help you regain your freedom

Marilyn: Thank you..I have been going through so much..I am about to lose my mind

Marlon: This is why we are here..To let you know that you are not alone..You have a whole team on your side

Chris: It is not going to be an easy battle..But we can win it..It is not going to be easy..Because the state will try everything in its power to make an example out of this case

Marlon: What Chris said is true..They want to set a precedent..Therefore..We have to be prepared

Marilyn: I really appreciate your help..You met my boyfriend?

Marlon: No Chris and I did not meet with him yet

Chris: When he was on his way to the office..We were on our way here to see you

Marlon: This is how committed we are..We don't waste any time at all

Marilyn: When do we expect to go to trial?

Marlon: First..I have to go to the bail hearing..To ask the judge to grant you bail..It will be a better situation for you

Chris: I just received a text..The hearing will be tomorrow

Marilyn: If I am granted bail..I will be able to go home..Right?

Marlon: Yes..And return to court the day of the trial

Marilyn: That would be a much better situation for me..It is so loud here at night..I can't sleep

Chris: It is not easy

Marilyn: Everybody is flushing their toilets

Chris: Yes..You are not alone..Many of our previous clients complained about that..What it is..The inmates use their toilets at night for some privacy..No other inmates are walking around

Marilyn: I figured that what it was..I haven't used the toilet since I've been in here

Marlon: It is normal..Your body shut down for a while..So..Tomorrow we go to the hearing..And we will go from there..How do you feel?..Is there anything issue regarding the jail that you want us to address?

Marilyn: I am fine..Not fine but..The only thing is the noise at night

Chris: What about your medications..You are able to take them

Marilyn: The nurse keeps them and every morning I go to the nurse and take my medications

Chris: Just got a text from Marvin..He wants me to ask you if you know Kim

Marilyn: Kim..Kim..I only know one Kim..And we are best friend..She is a brunette

Chris: She said she knows you

Marilyn: Yes..I know Kim since elementary school..We are in fact best buddies

Chris: The world is very small place..Isn't it?

Marilyn: Yes it is

C.O.: Who are you here to see ma'am?

Kim: Marilyn..Marilyn Winter

C.O.: I believe she is meeting with her lawyers right now

Kim: I know the lawyers..It's ok for me to join them

C.O.: Let me ask the inmate if it's ok

Kim: No problem

C.O.: Ma'am..You have another visitor..Do you want her to join you?

Marilyn: Who is it?

C.O.: Her name is Kim

Marilyn: Kim is here..Yes..Yes..Let her in

Marlon: She came?

Chris: That's nice

C.O.: Over there please..At table ten

Kim: Thank you

Marilyn: Hey you?..What are you doing here? Are you pregnant too?

Kim: Very funny..I am here for refusing to be pregnant..That's inverse of yours

Marilyn: I see..You know those guys?

Kim: If I know those guys?..What do you mean? Those guys are always blowing up my phone

Marlon: Not me Kim..I am a married man

Kim: Well..Not you but Chris and Marvin..They called me all the time..Inviting me on dates

Chris: You already know..We are gentlemen..We don't want you to be bored

Kim: Yeah right..Please..Chris I am not here to see you

Chris: It's ok..I can wait

Kim: You can wait?..How are you doing Lyn?

Marilyn: I feel much better now..I am not alone in this

Kim: No you are not..And you have the best team on your side

Marlon: We really need to get ready for battle..The state is going all out in this

Chris: I believe so too..What we are trying to say Marilyn..This is case is not necessarily about you..They want to use you as precedent..As an example

Marlon: That's right..By that we mean..They are going to use all their resources..Their best prosecution team in order to obtain a conviction

Kim: Why they even think that they have the right to decide what a woman does with her body?

I just don't get it

Marilyn: It's insane

Marlon: We must be prepared to move quick..Not giving them the time to get ready

Chris: This never really works against a prosecution's team ..They have the resources to match your speed..This time it's going to be a team so strong..Beyond the realm of their imagination

Kim: Really?..Who do you guys have on board?

Chris: It's big

Kim: Who are they?

Marlon: You want me to tell her Chris?

Kim: What is it top secret?

Chris: I will tell her..We line a large group of women..Because this is a case that concerned all women

Kim: Who is on the team already Chris?

Chris: Oh my god Kim..You are still nosey

Marlon: Tell her Chris

Kim: It is not being nosey..I just want to know

Marilyn: They know you well Kim

Kim: Lyn..I thought you were on my side

Marilyn: I am..You are not nosey..You simply have an investigative mind

Marlon: That's a very nice way to put it

Kim: Whatever guys..Are you going to tell me or not?

Chris: Ok..Sure..The ladies are..Of course Khlo..Renee

Kim: Wait a minute..I know both of them

Chris: We know that..You know everybody..You are the most popular person in town

Kim: But..None of those two are defense lawyers

Marlon: Kimberly..C'mon..You need to update your info..Khlo switched from prosecutor to defense

Kim: Renee is a business lawyer

Chris: Not anymore..She is a defense attorney now..Well..She is still a business lawyer but also defense lawyer

Kim: They are both smart ladies..Who else you guys have on board?

Chris: We also have Kourt and Malika..Even though we haven't contacted Kourt yet..I am sure she will be pleased to join the team

Kim: I am so jealous..I should not have gotten in the fashion industry..I would have been in court pacing it out with those ladies

Chris: No..You don't mean it..You have one of the biggest and most known fashion agencies

Kim: Well..I am doing ok..Knock on wood..My girls are walking all over the world..Fashion designers are blowing my phone days and night..My girls are completely booked

Marlon: Wow

Chris: How many you have now

Kim: I have one hundred and fifty five models..They are in majority top models..The best baby

Chris: That's the money lady right here

Marilyn: I remember when Kim started..Just a few years ago

Kim: Right..Just with three girls..And the designers loved them and kept asking me for more girls..So my agency caught fire

Marilyn: Yep

Kim: I worked so hard to meet the demand..In business this is something you must know..When you are catching fire..You must get ready to throw wood into it at that time..Otherwise you will miss the opportunity

Marlon: That's absolutely right..This is why a lot of people passed on..On great talents..They waited too long until someone else come along and swipe the artist away

Chris: You are right..You have to be willing to take risk when you see someone with talent..Because you blink and he or she is gone..And just have to watch him or her blows up into a phenomenon

Marlon: This is so true..Do you know how many people passed on Marshall?

Marilyn: Who is Marshall?

Kim: Eminem the rapper

Chris: They saw his talent but they were not willing to take the risk..Until somebody signed him

Marlon: It's always like that..But in your case Kim..It was a little different..Right?

Kim: Well..The designers realized that I had the eyes to spot a great model..They started to ask me for girls..And I only had three..I was working my girls to death

Marilyn: I remember that..Kim would be on the phone postponing..Asking for more time

Kim: You remember?..I only had three girls

Marlon: How did you grow from three to one hundred fifty in such a short time?

Kim: Well would be walking in the streets recruiting girls..If I saw someone with great potential..I would give her my card and a check of a check of a thousand dollars on the spot

Chris: Really?

Kim: Yes..I would tell her..You come to my office to sign up and you can cash that check

Marlon: You were a beast

Kim: I don't play..I did not go to business school for no reason

Marlon: That is not learned in school

Chris: She is a natural hustler

Kim: Yep..You can say that..I had girls line in my office..I did not have enough space..So I started to meet them at my apartment

Marlon: It was brilliant

Kim: The designers were satisfied..And the money start to come in

Chris: Hustler baby..Who's phone is ringing?

Marlon: That's mine..That's Khlo..Hello

Khlo: Hello Marlon

Marlon: How are you..I am glad you called..We are having a meeting next week

Khlo: This is exactly why I am calling..I don't think I will be able to be in that case

Marlon: Really?..Why?..You got cold feet..You would do well

Khlo: I am sorry..Something comes up..I have to train for a marathon..I will be spending a lot of time with the trainer..He will leave town in a hurry in a couple weeks so that's the only time I have to train with him..I am sorry

Marlon: Chris..You heard that..Khlo will not be in this case

Chris: Who cares about Khlo..We will replace her by another beautiful lady..You know how we do..I am kidding..What's wrong?..Why?..Let me talk to her..Hello

Khlo: Hello..Chris?

Chris: Yeah..I am disappointed in you..I thought you were more serious..The real deal is dropped on your lap and you are backing down..Shame on you

Khlo: Chris..Chris..Hear me out before you start to bash me

Chris: I don't care about your excuses..This is the time for you to grow some balls Khlo and make the right decision..You don't come with us this time..You know it's over between us..You can forget about being part of the dream team

Khlo: Chris..Chris please..I did not call to talk to you

Chris: You know I said what's on my mind..Here we have the biggest case of the decade coming up..The opportunity of a life time to show your long legs..Pacing the courtroom..Dropping knowledge and make the whole world stop..The opportunity to get the world glue to their television sets..You are saying you can do it..You know what..I am done with you

Khlo: Did Marlon tell you why?

Chris: No..He did not tell me why..I heard he mentioned doing work with some stupid trainer..You prefer to spend time with some sweaty guy..Instead of coming into the courtroom with us..Let it be known Khlo..We are offering you an opportunity to rest your body and use your brain..The most beautiful thing..You know what?..No problem..I will call Kristen today..She will replace you

Khlo: Can I say something..I did not say categorically that I would not do it

Chris: Well..You don't have much time Khlo..Next week we are having attorney's meeting..You know how much we love you..But it's your choice to walk away..So..I can tell you right now..If we don't hear from you this weekend..You will be replaced by Kristen

Khlo: This is why I don't like talking to you..You are a hot head Chris

Chris: I am not a hot head..I say it the way it is..Get your stuff together or you will be watching our beautiful women on TV doing their stuff

Khlo: Can I please talk to Marlon

Chris: Listen

Khlo: Chris..Please..Let me talk to Marlon

Marlon: Yes..Quitter..You quit on me..I am your biggest supporter..I voted for you to be in the case..I wasted my vote

Khlo: I am not a quitter Marlon..You know me better

Marlon: Now is the time to prove it..And you chose to do otherwise..This case is the most important..Bigger than "The Family".."The Surgeon".."Good Deed"..We have my buddy Ron from the "Redeemed" and Vic from "The stranger is a Friend" coming in..It's going to be a ball..You bail out of that..That's insane..Another woman needs you to be in court to defend her and make history..You can't pass on something of this magnitude..I don't know what to say..You know me..I am more lenient than Chris and Marvin..Let us know what you chose to do..I thought our relationship meant more to you Khlo?

Khlo: You guys are killing me

Marlon: Wait until you hear from your biggest fan..Marvin..He is going to be so disappointed..Anyway..You have the weekend to think it over and let us know what you want to do

Marlon: You know we love you..To me it would have been the best opportunity for you to get your feet wet as a defense lawyer..Like they say..You can only take a donkey to the river but you can't force her to drink

Khlo: What are you saying Marlon?..Are you calling me a donkey?

Marlon: No..Not at all..It's a saying

Chris: Yes..She is a donkey for quitting on us

Khlo: Tell Chris to shut up

Marlon: You heard him in the background..Right?

Khlo: Yes..I heard his big mouth

Marlon: This is the fighting spirit we needed you to bring in the courtroom..Let us know Khlo..We still love you and we would love to have you

Chris: Don't talk to her like that..Tell her..Get it together or else

Khlo: Tell Chris hush..I will let you know Marlon

Marlon: The sooner the better..So we can sit down and plan how we are going to bring it to them..Take care

Khlo: I will talk to you soon..Where are you guys?

Marlon: We are at the jail with the client

Kim: Say hello to her for me Marlon

Marlon: Somebody said hello

Khlo: Who is it?

Marlon: Kim

Khlo: You guys know Kim?

Marlon: What do you mean? Kim is family to the dream team

Chris: You are the only stranger to the dream team

Khlo: Whatever Chris..Tell Kim I said hello..I will contact you soon Marlon

Marlon: No problem

Khlo: I can't believe you let Chris talk to me that way

Marlon: You know Chris..He is the way he is..He does not hold punches..He is my brother..I have no choice but to love the way he is..But you know how much we love you

Khlo: I am not sure now

Marlon: You already know..We are looking forward to hear from you

Khlo: Talk to you soon

Marlon: She is mad at you

Chris: Who?..Khlo?

Marlon: Yep

Chris: She is always mad at me anyway

Marlon: I think we are set..Marilyn..Do you have any question you would like me to answer?

Marilyn: No..Everything seems to be clear..We are going to trial as soon as possible

Marlon: Yes..But first..Tomorrow I have to go see the judge for the bail hearing

Chris: At what time it is?

Marlon: Most likely at ten..I will find out

Chris: Should we bring her?

Marlon: Not necessarily..Considering her health status..I think it's best not to bring her

Chris: You are right..The hearing can last many hours

Kim: Really?..Many hours?

Marlon: Ok guys..It's that time for us to leave..The C.O. is looking at me..We've been in here for a while..Ok..Marilyn..Take care..Call me anytime ok

Marilyn: Thank you..Thank you for bringing Kim

Chris: we did not bring Kim

Marlon: Kim is a good friend..She will find you where ever you are

Chris: Take care Marilyn..Don't worry..We are on it

Kim: Bye honey..I will be there..What do you want me to bring next time?

Chris: Kim..This is not the Hilton five stars hotel..What do you plan on bringing her..A fur coat?

Kim: It's not a bad idea..It's freezing in here..You are not coming to the hearing tomorrow?

Chris: The reason why she can't come Kim..The judge might have other hearings..So..We may have to wait many hours for our case to be heard

Kim: I see..I hope she gets bail..I can't stand seeing my friend with that orange jumpsuit..She did not do anything wrong but getting pregnant like any other woman..This is so wrong

Marlon: Bye..Let's go guys..Bye Marilyn

Marilyn: Bye

_Following those words..A female C.O. takes Marilyn by her arm and walks her back to her cell

Marlon: Well..We should not expect anything..It's a political case..They want to make an example out of her

Chris: Why don't we go to a restaurant..I am hungry

Marlon: That's not a bad idea..Where do you have in mind?

Chris: Let's go to the Tavern Noir..They serve drinks as well

Marlon: The food is not too bad

Kim: The food is good?

Chris: Yes Kim..The food is very good

Kim: I don't know..My pallet is pretty spoiled with the French cuisine

Chris: I know..Whatever Ms. Frenchie..This is America..Get back to eating your cheese burger

Kim: Actually..Cheese burger is my favorite

Marlon: I don't remember exactly where the place is Chris

Chris: Follow me guys

Marlon: No problem

Kim: Guys..Don't drive too fast

Chris: You just don't want to mess up your brand new car..Uh?

Kim: It's not that Chris..I am not into driving fast

Chris: It's nice..What kind of ride is it?

Kim: It's a gift from one of the designers..It's a Citroën..It could be the only one in America

Chris: Follow me..It's only a couple blocks away

_Five minutes later..They arrive at the restaurant

Kim: That's beautiful..I really like the décor

Chris: C'mon Kim..You have to trust me..You think I would take you to a place that's not fine

Marlon: That's Chris favorite spot..Let's sit right here..You like this seat?

Chris: It's ok

Marlon: Not you Chris..I was talking to the Kim

Chris: You already know wherever I sit here I am home

Kim: It's ok

Chris: Marlon..Is that your phone or mine?

Marlon: It's mine

Chris: Wifey is checking on you

Marlon: No..It's Khlo

Chris: Really?..Let me talk to her

Marlon: Leave her alone..She will beat you down Chris

Chris: I might like it

Marlon: Hello

Khlo: Hello..Marlon?

Marlon: Yes..It's me..How are you honey?

Khlo: I am fine..I am calling to let you know that I will be part of the team

Marlon: That's what I am talking about..I knew the love was real

Khlo: Now..I want your friend..Brother whatever he is to you..I want him to apologize to me

Marlon: Chris..Khlo wants an apology

Chris: No problem

Kim: I see..You guys have to be prepared for war

Chris: Exactly..War is the right word

Marlon: This is why we are trying to put together the most vicious team ever

Chris: We might have to call Vic and Ron

Marlon: That's not a bad idea

Kim: Who are they?

Chris: Where have you been Kim?..You don't know Ron and Vic?

Marlon: They are my buddies..Vic was in the "The Stranger Is A Friend" case and Ron was in the "Redeemed" case..They are very good

Kim: How good?..Better than you guys?

Chris: Same Kim..You come to court with us you will be destroyed

Kim: This is very serious...A group of how many lawyers you guys are going to bring in?

Marlon: Let me see..Chris..Marvin..Ron..Vic..Olivier and myself

Kim: Six lawyers

Chris: And the ladies..Don't forget the ladies

Kim: Who are they?

Marlon: Kourt..Malika..Renee..Khlo or Kristen

Chris: I believe Khlo will be there..I don't think she will pass on an opportunity as such

Marlon: To tell you the truth..I really want her to be there

Chris: This is why I was talking to her like that..Just to get under her skin..She is a fighter..Once she is pushed she is ready to fight

Marlon: I see..This is why you were talking that way to her?

Chris: Of course..I called her a quitter..She does not like challenges

Marlon: She is a rebel

Chris: Exactly..She is sweet though..And very loyal..When she is with you..She will do everything she can to make you happy

Kim: So..What happened Chris?..Why your relationship with her did not last?

Chris: It was my fault..She is too good for me..I was not ready for a serious relationship

Marlon: Chris is committed on being a player for life

Chris: Not really..I was feeling so bad..She would not talk to her male friends just not to hurt me..Everything I said she was willing to do..Very sweet person

Marlon: You don't find that kind of commitment every day

Kim: I think you still love her

Chris: Definitely

Kim: Guess what?..I think it's too late Chris

Chris: Why would you say that?

Kim: From what I heard..She in love with a writer

Marlon: I heard that too..She is an author herself..The love train left you Chris

Chris: Whatever guys

Marlon: Chris..Don't worry about that..The ladies are crazy about him..He is going to be player of the year

Chris: Not me..Marvin is player of the year..Excuse me..Can you bring something to eat here..So I can keep those two occupied..And get them off my back

Waiter: Yes sir..Are you ready to order?

Chris: I want two beers and two steak sandwiches

Marlon: Chris..You must really hungry

Kim: Chris..You can eat all that..Two steak sandwich

Marlon: Those two guys..Marvin and Chris..They don't play

Chris: Listen..Last week..Marvin and I went to the buffet place on Lenox Ave

Marlon: That's a beautiful place..And the food is very good

Chris: I thought they were going to ask us to leave..Just after workout at the gym..They were looking at us like

Kim: I saw that place but I've never been there

Chris: You should try it

Marlon: It's a little pricy for a buffet..It's sixty dollars each..But the place is beautiful..Free drinks

Chris: The food is really good

Kim: I am not much of an eater..I am watching my weight

Waiter: Are you ready to order?

Kim: Just a grill cheese sandwich

Waiter: What do you want to drink?

Kim: Sparkling water..Do you have Evian?

Waiter: Yes we do..What about you sir?

Marlon: Cheese steak sandwich as well

Waiter: You want two as well

Marlon: No..Just one..This guy here is in the big league of eater..Have you met his partner in crime Marvin?

Waiter: I am not sure

Chris: Of course..We came here all the time

Waiter: I think I know who you are talking about

Marlon: Just one sandwich and a beer

Waiter: what kind of beer

Marlon: A bud..Bottle please

Kim: When is the meeting?

Marlon: Tomorrow we have the bail hearing..Maybe tomorrow afternoon..What do you think Chris?..Chris..What do you think?

Chris: What?

Kim: He is lost in his phone..Busy texting..Who are you texting..That's so rude

Chris: Sorry guys..It was very important

Kim: Dinner tonight and cop it at my place..That's how important it was

Chris: No..Not that..It was business

Kim: Whatever..Marlon wants to know..Do you think having the meeting tomorrow after the hearing a good idea

Chris: I think it's perfect..We haven't heard from Kourt yet

Marlon: I talked to Kourt..She will be there..I guess we have to contact Renee

Chris: I will call Malika

Kim: Why are you so eager to call Malika Chris?

Chris: I am always a suspect in your eyes Kim

Kim: Not a suspect..But a player for sure..You know she is good friend with Khlo

Chris: Who you are telling?..They are so close..They are annoying..I remember one time I was talking to Khlo..Then Malika called her on the phone..She would not stop talking..So I said to her..Are you guys down for a threesome

Kim: You are so crazy Chris

Chris: I said it on purpose to get her attention

Marlon: What did she say?

Chris: She just looked at me and tried to kick me

Kim: Khlo is very open minded..She does not get offended by stuff like that..But don't take her for granted..She loves really hard..When she loves she really loves you..Nothing people say about you matters..She believes in you as if you are her world..But if you are unfaithful..You pushed her to break up with you..You stand no chance of winning her heart back

Chris: Are you trying to discourage me?

Kim: Not at all..I am just telling you what it is

Chris: She is a sweetheart

Kim: No doubt she is..You should have recognized it when you had the chance

Chris: Thank you for reminding me Kim

Kim: You are welcome

Marlon: Guys..The food looks really good..Kim..You have gotten a steak sandwich as well

Kim: No..It's too much for me..I have to be a good example for my girls..I will get a bite form yours

Marlon: No problem

Kim: Let me get it from Chris..He has two

Chris: Go ahead Kim

Kim: Look how he is watching me

Chris: Kim..Stop being funny..Take a bite already..Oh my god..I did not you could bite so big

Kim: You want me to buy another one Chris

Marlon: No Kim..Do not encourage him

Chris: A woman with a big bite is a great thing

Kim: Whatever Chris

Chris: Kim..Baby

Kim: What?

Chris: Your phone is ringing

Kim: Ok..Ok..Where is it?..Hello..Hey Khlo..Where are you?

Khlo: I am leaving the courthouse now..I am with Kourt and Renee

Kim: Why don't you stop by

Khlo: Where..You guys are still at the jail?

Kim: No..C'mon..We left a while ago..We are now at a restaurant..Come

Khlo: What's the name of the place?

Kim: I am not sure..Hold on..Let me ask Chris..Chris..What is the name of the place?

Chris: Tavern Noir

Kim: Tavern Noir

Khlo: He knows every place in town..Where is it?

Kim: It's on Lenox Ave

Khlo: I think I know where that is

Kim: The girls are coming?

Khlo: Who?..Kourt and Renee?

Kim: Yes

Khlo: I am not sure..Let me ask them..Guys..You want to come for a drink..The guys are at a place and want you to come

Kourt: Who is there?

Khlo: Kourt wants to know who is there

Kim: Who is there?

Khlo: You know Kourt..She has to know..Are you coming Renee?

Renee: I am coming but I can't stay too long..I have court in the morning

Khlo: We are coming

Kim: Hurry up..This guy Chris is out of control here..Chris your boss is coming

Chris: Who is that?..Khlo?

Khlo: I am not his boss Kim..Don't put idea in his head

Kim: Hurry up

Khlo: See you guys soon

_Meanwhile at the firm

Marvin: Did I cover everything?..Do you have any more questions for me?

Gary: Everything is clear..The bail hearing is for tomorrow..Then we will go from there

Marvin: Exactly

Gary: The money will be in the account tomorrow morning..Ok..Thank you so much

Marvin: You are welcome..See you..Take care

_At the restaurant

Kim: What take you guys so long?

Khlo: There was a little bit of traffic

Kim: At this time..It's true

Khlo: Hello everyone

Marlon: Where is my hug Khlo?

Khlo: How are you Marlon?

Marlon: I am fine..Hello Renee..Kourt..You changed your hair color

Renee: Hello Marlon..Hello Chris

Chris: My hair is the same..Well..I changed the color a while now..That's how long ago I saw you

Kourt: Chris is looking good

Chris: Good looking as usual

Khlo: Can you wait for someone to say it

Chris: No..I don't have to wait for anyone..I am the best judge of myself

Marlon: Excuse me..Can we put those two tables together?

Waiter: Sure..No problem..I will move them for you

Marlon: Thank you

Chris: We could have had the meeting here

Marlon: we are missing a few guys here

Khlo: Who is missing?

Marlon: Malika..Ron..Olivier and Vic

Kourt: I can't wait to see Vic

Khlo: Kourt is in love with Vic..She is too afraid to tell him

Kourt: Please Khlo..I never said that I was in love with him

Khlo: Excuse me..What did you say?

Kourt: I simply said that I like him

Chris: He will be here

Renee: How many people are on that team?

Marlon: I think nine

Chris: More than nine Marlon

Kim: More than nine?

Chris: Check it out..Marlon..Marvin..Vic..Ron..Olivier and Myself..That's six already

Khlo: Wow..It's all out war

Marlon: It is..We have to be prepared

Chris: Listen up guys

Waiter: Are you guys ready to order?

Khlo: Give us a couple of minutes please

Chris: Listen..The ladies are..Khlo..Malika..Renee and Kourt

Marlon: That's ten..Six men and four ladies

Kourt: I heard the prosecution is putting together a very strong team

Marlon: I would not doubt that

_Meanwhile at the district attorney office

D.A.: Good afternoon everyone..This meeting is regarding the upcoming trial regarding the refusal to end a risky pregnancy..We are all aware of that upcoming case..I call the meeting today..What seems to be very early considering the trial might be held in another three weeks..I want everyone to be prepared..I will put together the team that will represent the state..It has to be our very best..This case has no precedent...Therefore..We must make of this case the best precedent ever..I heard that the defense is putting together a very strong team..It is coming from the MMC Firm..I know what those guys can do..If you are not prepared..Do not go face them in the courtroom..They will certainly make you look bad..Having said that..Tomorrow morning..You will find out if you are in the team or not..Even if you are not in the team..Your assistance will be needed throughout the trial

Prosecutor: How many members the team will have?

D.A.: Ten members will not be an exaggeration..We are going in really deep..Jackson..I will need you in my office this afternoon

Jackson: At what time sir?

D.A.: Right after the meeting..Do you have any questions?

Henry: One needs to be a senior investigator to be in the team?

D.A.: Not necessarily..It's going to be a very emotional case..Considering the nature of the case..We will need a few women in the team..Also..I want to bring to your attention that Khlo will be..Well I don't want to say will be..But might be in the defense team

Jackson: Khlo..Who used to work here with us?

D.A.: Yes..It is a hear-say..I have no confirmation yet..This is to give you an idea how strong a team the defense is putting together..I don't know if you hear about the two brothers..Marlon and Marvin..Also Chris..I am just praying that Vic and Ron don't show up in that courtroom..We will be in real trouble..I know those guys..I know what they can do..Therefore..I want everyone of you to adopt a war mindset..Don't let anything flies..Don't be afraid to object..How many times that is necessary..We are going to be in a playoff series against that defense team..Nobody goes in the paint for layups..Do you understand me?

Jackson: Yes sir

D.A.: Why only Jackson answered me?..The rest of you are scared?

Phillip: No sir..We are not scared..It will be an honor to be part of the team

D.A.: I like your attitude Phillip..You might be..I like your pitch

Phillip: It was not a pitch sir

D.A.: C'mon Phillip..I was not born yesterday

_At the restaurant

Kim: Khlo..You look so good..You lost so much wait

Khlo: You think so..I love you for that

Renee: These days..I call her the queen

Kourt: Please Renee..Don't make her head bigger than it is

Khlo: Kourt always hating on me..She just love me too much

Chris: Who knew those two could become best friends?

Marlon: Who?

Chris: Kourt and Khlo

Khlo: Don't talk so fast mister mature man..I am not best friend with her..That is proof that you don't know me..You never tried to

Marlon: Wait a minute..You are coming at my brother a little strong here

Kim: I think they are still in love..Answer your phone Khlo

Khlo: Hello..Hey..Where are you? You are the only one missing

Malika: Missing from what?

Khlo: All the guys are here..Well..Marlon and Chris..Kim..Renee and Kourt

Malika: what is the occasion..The lawyers' meeting is today?

Khlo: No..We are at the Taverne Noir

Malika: Chris is there? ..I don't want to talk to him

Chris: Why?

Malika: Since you guys broke up..I haven't talk to him since

Khlo: No..Don't make it a big issue..You know Chris will be Chris

Chris: Why you guys talking about me..Who is this?

Khlo: Malika

Chris: Give the phone

Khlo: Chris..You can just take my phone from my hand..You don't pay the bill

Chris: Hello

Malika: What Chris?..What do you want?

Chris: I want to know why you are talking about me

Malika: Nobody was talking about you..Don't flatter yourself

Chris: Are you coming here or not?

Malika: I am not sure

Chris: Well..Whenever you decide..Your favorite seat is reserved

Malika: What sit would that be Chris?

Chris: My lap baby

Malika: Chris..Stop already

Chris: You know I have nothing but love for you..Come here and everything is on me

Malika: everything like what Chris?

Chris: Food..Drinks

Malika: I can buy my own food and drinks

Chris: Well..Paintings that are on the walls..You can't buy them..They are not for sale

Malika: This is not your place..How are you going to give them to me?

Chris: You get here..Listen Malika..Can you stop at my place and pick something for me

Malika: No..I am not going to your place..I don't have the key to your place

Chris: The door has a code..I can give it to you

Malika: No..I am almost there..At the restaurant anyway..Bye Chris..Let me talk to my friend

Chris: Here is your friend..See you soon

Malika: He does not change

Khlo: Not at all..Everything is a joke to Chris..He does not take anything seriously..You are almost here?

Malika: Yes

Kim: Let me talk to her

Khlo: She is almost here Kim

Marlon: Guys..I have good news..I just received a snap from my guys..They are both coming

Renee: Who?

Marlon: Ron and Vic

Chris: They texted you?

Marlon: No..Vic sent me a snap

Chris: That's good stuff

Renee: Guys..I am sorry..I might have to leave now

Chris: C'mon Renee..You just got here

Marlon: She has to be in court early morning

Chris: Ok..I can respect that

Khlo: What case is it?

Renee: It's a murder case

Khlo: Wow..How is your client looking?

Renee: He has a great alibi..He has a receipt that proves that he was at a store miles away from the crime scene when the crime was committed

Khlo: Do they have any video shots?

Kourt: Wow..I am impressed..Did you guys hear what question the rookie asked?

Khlo: Who is the rookie?

Kourt: You?

Marlon: Don't be fooled..Khlo is not a rookie when it comes to criminal cases

Khlo: Let her talk Marlon..You know how Kourt is already

Chris: There is not much deference between a prosecutor and a defense attorney

Renee: Right..You must have great knowledge in criminal law to be a prosecutor or a defense lawyer

Khlo: That's all..So..I don't see where the rookie came from?

Renee: Why she called you a rookie anyway?

Khlo: Because I used to be a prosecutor..I just started to work as a defense lawyer

Kourt: Say it right Khlo..It's a going to be your first job as a defense lawyer

Khlo: It does not matter..Everything I do I do it well..Check my record..I did not lose a case

Kourt: Not so fast..You lost one

Khlo: Which case you are referring to.."A Good Deed"?

Kourt: It's only because the prosecution office gave me a witness who committed perjury on the stand

Chris: I heard the story Kourt..She was up your neck every day in that courtroom

Marlon: I stopped by once..They were killing each other..The judge had enough of their catfight

Kim: How in the world you guys become best friends

Khlo: Who said I am best friend with her

Kourt: She is in love with me

Renee: I really think that you guys love each other too much

Khlo: Wrong

Renee: Ok guys..I have to go

Marlon: Renee..Don't forget the meeting is for tomorrow

Renee: Sure..No problem..I will be available in the afternoon..Malika is here

Malika: Hello Renee..It's been such a long time

Renee: Right..Right...But I will be seeing you every day..You are on the case..Right?

Malika: Yes..Hello everybody

Khlo: You took forever to get here

Malika: I am here Khlo..That's what count

Khlo: But..You are late

Malika: Late to what?..You guys had the meeting?..I thought the meeting was tomorrow

Marlon: Don't worry Malika..Khlo is just messing with you

Chris: The meeting is for tomorrow..Don't be late..That's what Khlo was trying to say

Malika: Chris if you could just not talk to me..I will appreciate it

Chris: That's what you said..Right Khlo?

Khlo: Don't put word in my mouth..I did not say that

Marlon: Chris..C'mon man..You expect to get between those two

Malika: I know..He is so crazy

Chris: I know Mo..I got no love from them..This is the best tag team ever

Kim: She was in love with you..And you took it for granted

Chris: Whatever Kim

Kim: That's your answer

Chris: What do you want me to say?..I don't live in the past

Marlon: Leave my brother alone..C'mon guys..By now you guys should know Chris..He is a great guy..But he just does not feel ready to commit

Malika: This is nonsense..In the process he is hurting so many women

Chris: Y'all are talking as if I invented heart break

Khlo: You did not invent it but you sure get yourself a license to use it

Chris: Oh my god..What is this? Some type of lynching?

Marlon: You are lucky I am here Chris..They would have done just that

Chris: You right about that

Kim: You are right..That's what he deserves

Chris: C'mon Kim..I thought you were on my side?

Kim: Not against my sister Khlo..You broke her heart

Marlon: Chris..Just apologize

Chris: Marlon..I don't think apology can fix that level of hatred

Malika: Nobody hates you..We just don't like what you do to the women

Chris: What did I do?

Kourt: You got them committed and then you break up with them

Chris: I never asked anyone for commitment..Khlo..Did I ask you for commitment?

Khlo: Are you talking to me?..This conversation is not about me..Because it has been so long..I don't even remember dating you

Marlon: Chris..She said she is over you

Chris: I am glad to hear that..I hope the whole crew could feel the same way

Marlon: My brother is a crazy guy

Chris: I Think..They love me too much

Marlon: I think so too

Chris: Khlo..You are just arguing..You haven't ordered anything yet

Kim: You are trying to change the subject

Chris: What subject?..Please waiter

Waiter: Yes

Chris: Bring them some food for me please

Kourt: Answer your phone Chris..You know it's your phone..Don't act as if you did not hear it..One of your heart break victims

Marlon: No..That's my phone

Chris: See..Always blaming Chris

Marlon: That's Marvin

Kim: Tell him to get here..He is my favorite guy

Marlon: Hello

Marvin: He bro..What's going on?..Only now I am leaving the office

Marlon: Really?..What don't you join us..We a have a lot of ladies right here

Marvin: Aren't Chris there?

Marlon: Yes he is

Marvin: They will be well taking care of

Marlon: This is not the case..He needs your help

Marvin: Really?..Usually Chris does not need help with the ladies

Marlon: He does this time..He needs a bodyguard

Marvin: I can't believe that..Who are the ladies?

Marlon: Khlo..Malika..Kourt and Kim..Renee was here as well..She just left

Marvin: He might need help

Marlon: They are asking for you..By the way how things went regarding the meeting with Gary?

Marvin: Everything went well..Ready to go

Marlon: Great..Are you coming?..Come get a drink with the ladies

Chris: You don't have to beg Marvin to come get a drink with the ladies

Marvin: What Chris said?

Marlon: He said..You don't have to force Marvin to come to the ladies

Marvin: Tell him help is on the way..Where are you guys?

Marlon: At the Taverne Noire

Kim: Is he coming?

Chris: Yes..Yes Kim he is coming..You want me to announce it in the loud speaker

Kourt: Don't be so jealous Chris

Chris: You must be crazy

Malika: You sounded like it

Chris: I am not the jealous type..Tell them Mo

Marlon: He is not the jealous type guys..He can dish and take it as well..I remember..He had a girlfriend..She was cheating and he knew about it and never said a thing to her

Chris: For what..I did not care..As long that I could see her when I wanted to

Marlon: He is not the jealous type guys

Malika: Yay..Marvin is here

Kim: Come sit next to me my love

Marlon: What's going on bro?

Marvin: I am good bro..My playboy brother Chris..How are you?

Chris: Same..Dealing with the hatred

Marvin: Tell me about it..How are my sweethearts doing?

Kim: We just miss you

Marvin: Khlo..Why you so quiet?

Marlon: She is in war mode

Marvin: With whom?

Chris: With me

Marvin: No time for that..It's time to have some fun..Come together as a team..And get ready to battle the prosecution

Marvin: I heard the D.A. has a lot of females on his team

Marlon: I would not be surprised

Kourt: It is a very strategic move..They want the jury to believe in their arguments

Khlo: We have to get ready..And go at them with the most

Malika: Khlo..You know them..Right?

Khlo: I know them..They are pretty good..Not better than us..There is one of them..She is a senior prosecutor..Her name is Jasmine..She is really good..Very aggressive

Marlon: Aggression is the key

Chris: We have to object as much as we can

Kourt: That should be the norm..Do not let them leave an imprint in the jury's mind

Malika: What about closing and opening arguments?

Marlon: We can all do a bit..I would love Ron to do one

Chris: Definitely..Ron should do one

Khlo: What about Vic?

Marlon: Yes..I think we are ready..We have enough players..That team is going to be intimidating

Marvin: Definitely

Marlon: Tomorrow during the meeting..We will lay out how we are going to proceed

_Meanwhile

Gary: Hello

Mindy: Hello Gary..It's me Mindy..Have you heard from Marilyn?

Gary: Yes..I am going to the hospital right now to see her

Mindy: Gary..I am a mother..I have a feeling something is wrong..Something terrible happened to my child

Gary: I can hear you

Mindy: C'mon Gary..I know you can hear me..Tell me the truth..What happened to Lyn?

Gary: Uh..Uh..I will stop by and talk to you Mindy

Mindy: Is she going to be ok?..I want to go to the hospital

Gary: I am on my way to your house

Mindy: Ok..You will take me to the hospital?

Gary: I am coming right now..See you soon

_A few minutes later Gary arrives at Mindy's home..He pulls into the driveway..His mind is racing..He does not know what he is going to tell Mindy yet..She does not know Marilyn is HIV positive..She does not know Marilyn is pregnant..And she is does not know Marilyn is in jail for being pregnant..All the stress that Gary has been dealing with started to affect his health..He has not been taking hi medicine..He is only concerned about Marilyn's wellbeing..He sits in the car for a while..He feels light headed..Tears start to run down his face..He wipes his face..As he looks up.. The front door opens and Mindy waves him in with a hand movement..He gets out the car very slowly..One leg at a time..He walks very slowly towards Mindy..With his head down in an attempt not to make eyes contact with Mindy..He can barely walk a straight line due to the dizziness..Let's listen:

Mindy: Hello Gary..How are you son?

Gary: Not too well Mindy..Not too well

_Gary feels that he is about to pass out..The virus is taking over his body..The stress..The worry of protecting Marilyn..And not taking care of himself begin to affect him

Mindy: You don't look too well

Gary: Can I have a glass of water please Mindy?

Mindy: Sure..Sure..Come with me

_Gary walks slowly in the hallway toward the kitchen..His hand along the wall so he does not fall..He finally makes it to the kitchen..He sits on the nearest chair he finds..He is in and out of consciousness..He sees Mindy as a blur..But yet..He is still trying to maintain his composure not to get Mindy panicky

Gary: Thank you Mindy

Mindy: You want smoothing to wipe your face..You are sweating a bit

Gary: Yes please

Mindy: You really look sick Gary..Is this because of Marilyn's situation?

Gary: Well..That too..But..I am a bit tired as well

Mindy: You want some orange juice

Gary: No thank you Mindy..I am fine

Mindy: How is Marilyn?

Gary: Well..She is not at the hospital Mindy

Mindy: Where is she then?..Where is my daughter?

Gary: She is in jail

Mindy: In jail? What d you mean?..For what?..We have to get her out

_Marlon..Chris and Marvin are at the courthouse for the bail hearing

Judge: Good morning..Counselors..Do you have any other motions..Well..Not motions but any request that you would like the court to consider at this time

Marlon: No your honor

Judge: If you don't have any request..Let hear your argument for your client's bail..Proceed please

Marlon: Thank you your honor..Your honor..We are here in front of this court this morning..Not only as lawyers but as guardians..We stand before you today not only in defense of our client..But also to put a stop to invasion of liberty..We are here your honor not to waste the tax payers' money..But to be the pioneers to a movement..To be the pioneer that will say enough is enough..Our client was arrested and thrown in jail just because she is pregnant..This is the year two thousand sixteen..No other women that I know of..Have been incarcerated because they were pregnant..Our client is the first victim..We stand before you today your honor..With the full confidence that bail will be granted to her..Simply because she should not have gotten arrested in the first place..Simply because we are living in America the land of the free..The opposition argued that our client is infected with a disease..Therefore she should end her pregnancy..Claiming that the infant will be infected and will die as a result..The state proposed solution is to end the pregnancy in order to prevent the infant's death..In other words..The State proposed killing the baby before he or she is born as a solution..Your honor..One does not have to be a rocket scientist or an avid humanitarian to realize that the state is traveling a wrong path by a proposition..Our argument is not an empty one..We can't afford to let the state set such a precedent..To accept such injustice your honor..It would be the same as providing ammunitions to an immoral cause that has no regards to the standards of which this country stands for..Not only that your honor..Medical records indicated that the percentage of infants' death from an infected mother is very minimal..So..Your honor..This is only an attempt of the state to interfere and control people's lives..We believe our client deserves to be with her family and get ready for the trial..There are in fact no reasons why she should be detained..She is not a flight risk your honor..She is also pregnant adding to her medical condition..At home will be a better place for her..So..She could rest comfortably and receive the proper care..We are confident your honor..That you will grant bail to our client..Which she desperately needs and so obviously deserves..Thank you your honor

Judge: Thank you..I heard of you guys from the M,M&C Firm..Very eloquent..But..Today there is one thing I have to make you guys understand..Granting bail to your client is not as simple as you may think..If it was for me..If it was solely based on morality..Compassion..It would have been an easy decision to make..But..We must understand the state position..The state has no intention to keep your client in jail..But the state has the ultimate duty to detain the unborn child..The state as taken possession of the unborn child..Since we can't separate the two..How do we do this?..What do you propose counselor?

Marvin: Your honor..We can only offer justice as a proposition..By that I mean..We must follow what the constitution proposed

Judge: Let me stop you right there counselor..This case has no precedents..When the constitution was created we certainly did not have those types of young women living such promiscuous and drugs filled life

Chris: Your honor with all due respect..I will ask you kindly to hold your defamatory horses..Our client is a very decent young woman..As decent as your daughter

Judge: Are you attacking my family?

Marvin: No your honor..Not at all..My colleague is simply trying to make you understand and see our client through the same lenses that you see your daughter..We must treat others the way we want to be treated..Refer and address others the way we wish to be addressed

Judge: This is a well prepared tag team uh?..I want to remind you that this is my courtroom..I am the king is this castle here..No one..Will come here and disrespect me

Chris: We understand that your honor..We are not by any mean intending to challenge your power in your courtroom..We are only trying to remind the judges that the courtrooms were created to find justice for the people..The courtrooms are also maintained financially by the tax payers..We are not here to disrespect..Nor to beg..We are here to ask or remind those it may concern to apply what is said in the constitution

Judge: I already mentioned to you that this case has no precedents..The state..Therefore can use its own discretion on how it handles it

Marvin: Your honor..With all due respect to your statement..I must remind you that invasion of civil liberty is not a right granted to any state by the constitution..Therefore..For a state to order a woman to abort her baby..It's a bit much your honor..If we set this as precedent..The state will soon tell people when to engage in sexual relations in their bedrooms

Judge: I heard of you guys..You are very skilled attorneys..But..There is one thing..One question on the table..You have not provided me with an answer to that question yet..That is..How do you separate the mother from the unborn baby..The state has taken possession of the unborn child

Marlon: Your honor we are not here to answer question for the state..We are simply here to ask you to grant bail to our client..Not as a favor but as a right that she has based on the law of the land..Based on the circumstances..Our client should be qualified for bail

Judge: I am not going to drag this any longer and waste tax payers' money..The state will remain in possession of your client..Well..Not client I should say..Rather in possession of the unborn child..And..Since we cannot separate the two..Your client will also be detained..Now you still can do what the law grants..That is to have a jury trial..Having said that..My decision is final..The accused will be detained until the trial..No bail will be granted..Thank you

_The next day at the M,M&C Firm..The lawyers meeting is about to start

Marlon: Look who is here

Vic: Hey brother..How are you? Long time no see..I called you this morning..You did not answer your phone

Marlon: I know..I was in court for the bail hearing

Vic: Did you get bail?

Marlon: No..The judge was the meanest Judge I have ever seen

Vic: Wow..It's ok..They can't hold her forever..The freedom machine is on the way

Marlon: Definitely.. Still looking good..Like the old days when you used to run over the defense players on the football field

Vic: Those days are long gone

Marlon: For you to say..You look like a rock..How is dad?..My man John..How is he doing?

Vic: Dad is fine..Same old John

Marlon: He is still running the shelter?

Vic: Call it a shelter if you want to..It's a five stars hotel

Marlon: I heard about it

Vic: That's the way dad is..He gives people his very best always

Marlon: That's what's up..How is Albert doing?

Vic: Al is fine..Still looking sharp

Marlon: He is still a lawyer?

Vic: Yes he is..He had lost his license..I helped him regained it..Now..He is working as a youth counselor

Marlon: I see

Vic: Nobody is here yet?

Marlon: You are the first to arrive my brother..Always early

Vic: This is a discipline I got since I was young..From being a scout..And playing football as well..You have to be there on time or coach will destroy you

Marlon: I know..Here's Marvin

Vic: That's Marv

Marvin: My brother

Vic: What's up bro?

Marvin: You

Vic: That's the way you pull up..What kind of ride?

Marvin: It's a BMW

Vic: Very nice..Where is the player of the year?

Marlon: Who?

Vic: You know who I am talking about..Chris

Marlon: Marvin is the player of the year

Vic: Really?..Where is Chris?

Marlon: He should be here soon

Vic: Considering the nature of the case..You guys should add some ladies to the team

Marvin: Of course we have some ladies in the team..Wait until you see the lineup

Vic: Really?..The finest attorneys in town

Marlon: Finest in every way

Vic: Ok..Can't wait to see that..Chris picked them?

Marvin: They are mostly friends..They are a bunch a beauty and great skills when it comes to litigation

Vic: That's Ron over there I saw his car

Marvin: Which one? That blue Benz?

Vic: Yep

Marlon: Get out of the car

Ron: Where do I park?

Marlon: Anywhere you want my brother

Ron: What's going on guys?..Am I late?

Marvin: No..You are not

Ron: I saw everybody outside I thought I was late..How is everybody doing?

Marlon: He still looks good

Ron: This physics..I got it in the penitentiary..Even when I was playing football at Kansas University I was not that big

Vic: You are right..I remember Ron used to ask me..How do you get so big?

Marlon: Are you ready for war guys?..By the way how is my girl Ashley doing?

Ron: Ashley is fine

Marvin: You guys still lives at Eagle Town?

Ron: I don't think I will ever leave Eagle Town..Born and raised there..When I had gotten in trouble..The people showed me a lot of support

Vic: You were the star there

Ron: So were you in your town Vic

Vic: Not as popular as you were.. How is Tony doing?

Ron: Tony is fine..He is a doctor

Marlon: Who is Tony?

Vic: The guy who had gotten stabbed during the fight in the bathroom..You remember the "Redeemed" case?

Marlon: Yes..I remember..I was in college at the time

Ron: It was a bad situation..But At the end of the day..I became a lawyer and motivational speaker..And me and Tony are really good friends

Vic: That's a beautiful thing

Ron: How is your dad..John?

Vic: My dad is fine

Ron: I was there at the opening of the shelter

Vic: I remember that

Ron: He is a great speaker

Vic: He is alright

Ron: How is your Linda doing?

Vic: My mom?..She is ok

Marlon: I think the ladies are arriving

Ron: Who is this in that Range Rover?

Marvin: That's Brianna

Vic: She looks so fine..Wow..Chris must love it..I know he loves women

Marvin: He tried..But she is not into playing game..She broke up with him

Brianna: Good morning..Good morning everyone

Marlon: Good morning my darling..Looking lovely as usual

Brianna: Who are all these fine men?

Marvin: It's me Marvin..And

Brianna: I know who you are Marvin..I am talking about these two right here

Vic: I am Victor

Brianna: Victor..The famous running back

Vic: That's what they say

Brianna: What are we doing..Are we going to play football..Or a litigation?

Marvin: Wait until you hear this one..This is Ron..The star running back from KU

Brianna: Who am I a cheerleader?..You guys look so fine..I would cheerlead for you anytime

Vic: Thank you..You look stunning yourself

Ron: Marlon..Are you sure we are here for a lawyers' pre trial meeting or a fashion show?

Brianna: Thank you

Marvin: I am so jealous of all the attention those two guys are getting

Brianna: No need to get jealous my love..You know I love you

Marlon: Where are the other girls?

Brianna: I don't know

Vic: That's my man Chris in that Corvette?

Marlon: Yep

Chris: What's going on here?

Vic: You..It's all about you playboy

Chris: Oh my god..I saw you guys here I thought I was pulling up in front of G.Q.

Marvin: Yes..G.Q. models on break time

Chris: That's what it looks like..What's going on big Ron?

Ron: I am fine brother..Nice to see you

Chris: Look who is here..Mister Victor..How are you?

Vic: Fine..I am here to come see you in order to sharpen my player skills

Khlo: You are so right about that

Chris: Please guys..Don't push me under the bus here

Marvin: Under the tiger you should say

Marlon: Don't start anything guys..This is not the time..We are here to do work as a team

Khlo: Under the tiger?..You guys have the wrong idea about who I am as a person

Marvin: The other ladies are here guys

Marlon: No me Khlo..I know you are the sweetest person

Kourt: Who is the sweetest person?

Khlo: Why don't you say good morning first Kourt..Then you will find out who the sweetest person is

Kourt: I know it's not you

Marlon: I beg to differ

Kourt: I am only kidding guys..She is the sweetest until she gets inside the courtroom

Marvin: That's the way it should be

Ron: Once in the courtroom..This is war

Renee: Good morning everyone

Chris: Good morning Renee..She is my favorite

Marvin: Stay away from her Chris

Chris: What do you mean?..She is my sister

Renee: Chris is my big brother

Chris: Tell them Renee

Marlon: Guys..Let's not waste anymore time..Let's go in

Marvin: Where is Malika?

Kourt: She is trying to park her car

Khlo: You right about that..She is trying

Malika: I heard you Khlo..Always have something to say about my driving

Khlo: You know I love you sister

Marlon: Guys..Let's go into the war room..Who's phone is ringing?

Brianna: That's mine

Chris: We have to turn all the phones off

Brianna: Hush Chris..Hello

Kim: Hello..Brianna..How are you?..What are you guys up to..Isn't the meeting today?

Brianna: Yes it is

Kim: Everybody is there?

Brianna: Yes..Everybody..The whole team

Kim: What about Ron and Vic?

Brianna: They are here as well..I never see so many good looking guys in one place

Kim: Maybe I should stop by

Brianna: You should never have gone into business..You see?

Kim: It's ok..I get to travel..And I really love what I do

Brianna: Why don't you stop by?

Kourt: Who is this on the phone?

Brianna: That's Kim

Kourt: Say hello to her for me

Brianna: Kourt says hello

Kourt: You know if Kim gets here no work will be done

Brianna: They say if you come no work will be done

Kim: That's not true..How could Kourt say such thing about me?

Kourt: The guys will be distracted by you

Brianna: You heard what she said?

Kim: I heard her..I will come anyway..I will bring lunch for you guys..But first I have to go to the jail to see Marilyn

Renee: Kim is such a sweetheart..She is going to the jail

Kim: Thank you Renee..I am on speaker I could hear everybody talking

Brianna: You've been on speaker from the very beginning

Malika: Marlon..I have the books

Chris: What books?

Malika: The reference books

Marlon: We will need to do a search on precedents

_The meeting was a success..The trial day is fast approaching..Gary health has deteriorating a bit..He was hospitalized for a week..Kim visits her friend Marilyn in jail..Let's listen

Marilyn: I did not know you were coming today?

Kim: I told you so..The last time I was here..You just don't remember

Marilyn: My memory is not great at all

Kim: You lost so much weight..Are you eating at all

Marilyn: I know..The medications cause me to lose weight..Also..I have morning sickness

Kim: Really?..You might be losing too much body fluid..It might put the baby in jeopardy..You have to try to eat Lyn

Marilyn: The food is not the greatest..This is jail Kim..This is not a five stars..The breads have molds on them

Kim: This is so wrong..If you detained people..Take away their freedom..They should at least be treated with dignity

Marilyn: I am so worried

Kim: Why?

Marilyn: I haven't heard from Gary in a week..He probably gave up..If he did I would understand

Kim: Why would you say that?..He does not strike me as such..I called him sometimes this week..He did not answer his phone..I know he has school work to do..I did not make a big deal out of it

Marilyn: No..I don't hear from him either..I am so worried..Maybe something happened to him

Kim: I don't think so..What could have happened to him?

Marilyn: He could be in the hospital

Kim: Why would he be..He seems very healthy

Marilyn: Did I tell you what he did?

Kim: What?

Marilyn: He got himself infected on purpose

Kim: On purpose?..What do you mean on purpose?

Marilyn: With the virus..So he could buy the medications for me..I would have been dead right now

Kim: You mean..He got infected to buy the medications for you

Marilyn: Yes..I did not have insurance coverage..My job did not offer any

Kim: He did that?..Oh my god Lyn..You let him do that?

Marilyn: C'mon Kim..You know me better..I did not know..He did not tell me anything..Until I see him bringing medications for me

Kim: Wow..That's a very kind thing he did..But..It's very crazy..He could die

Marilyn: Especially..He has not been taking good care of himself..I kept telling him to take the medications..He does not listen..I want you to go to the hospital to check if he is hospitalized for me please..Would you do that for me?

Kim: Of course..You want me to go now?

Marilyn: I would appreciate it..Thank you so much

Kim: C'mon Lyn..No need to thank me..I am with you in this..Ok..So let me get going..Which hospital he might be

Marilyn: Check Saint Jude..I don't think he would go to the one that is affiliated with this school..He would not want any of the students to see him there

Kim: Ok..I will go right now..I will let you know

Marilyn: Thank you so much

_Kim leaves the jail and heads to Saint Jude Hospital..She is there..And a nurse tells her the room number where Gary is

Nurse: He is at room number twelve

Kim: Thank you

_Kim walks very slowly..Knocks on the opened door very lightly..Then..Enters the room

Kim: Hi Gary..How are you?

_Gary looks at her for a good thirty seconds..He did not recognize her..Or he thought that he was dreaming

Gary: Kim..Is that you?

Kim: Yes..It's me..How are you?

Gary: Not too well..How do you find me?

Kim: It was not hard..Marilyn is worried..No one knows where you are

Gary: I was not feeling too well at all..I came in and the doctors kept me..Did Marilyn tell you?

Kim: Yes she did

Gary: Did she get bail?

Kim: No she did not

Gary: Oh god..She is still in jail?

Kim: Don't worry about that now..She is ok..She is going to trial next week..We are concerned about you now..My phone is ringing..That's Khlo

Brianna: Hello Kim

Kim: Yes

Brianna: Where are you?

Kim: I am at the hospital

Brianna: What's wrong?

Kim: I stop by to see Gary

Brianna: What is wrong with him?

Kim: It's a long story..Will talk to you when I see you

_It was the Sunday before the trial..The defense team members meet at a restaurant for a dinner party before the war..It's a very nice restaurant..One by one the team members arrive to the restaurant's parking lot..The valet service members open their doors and take their cars away..They look like movie stars..Getting out their fancy cars..Looking sharp..The first to arrive are Marlon and Marvin..Marlon get his brand new sports Jeep..Marvin slides out his BMW..As Marlon saying hello to Marvin..Chris pulls up in his brand new corvette..New hair cut..Wearing dark blue shirt dark pants with some alligators without any socks..This is Chris..Soon after Vic and Ron pull up..Vic is always a speed and muscles guys..He slowly opens the door of his twelve cylinders Mustang..Ron is more conservative..He drives a new Benz..Then girls begin to arrive

Kourt: Hello..Hello everyone

Chris: Hello Kourt..How are you?

Kourt: I am fine..Am I the first lady to arrive?

Vic: Yes you are

Kourt: I saw Khlo driving behind me..I don't know where she went

Marvin: You know what they say..The early bird gets the good worms

Kourt: In this case the early bird gets all the worms..Here are Renee and Khlo

Vic: The ladies look so good..You would think there is a fashion show going on out here

Ron: I concur..Three more cars are puling in..I think we are complete

Marlon: I think so

Brianna: That's Malika..And the black car is Kim

Chris: Kim is here

Marvin: Of course she is here..She is involved in every aspect of it..You need to remember..Marilyn is her best friend

Brianna: I know..Look at you..What a beautiful dress..Where did you buy it

Kim: France..At Nantes

Renee: I really love it

Marlon: Guys..Are we ready to go in?

Chris: Guys..As you enter the door take the stairs that are on the left

Brianna: We are going upstairs?

Chris: Yes..We are going upstairs

Renee: Are they going to have enough room for us upstairs?

Chris: The whole second floor is ours

Malika: Chris..You went all out

Chris: You already know me..It's all or nothing

Marvin: The owner is Chris' friend

Chris: C'mon Marv..What is this about?

Vic: He can't keep a secret..Can he Chris?

Chris: He messed my game

Kourt: What game Chris..Who are you trying to impress?

Kim: Maybe he is trying to win her back

Brianna: I hope you guys are not talking about me..Wow..This is a beautiful place

Chris: Thank you

Ron: I like that..Chris gracefully accepted the credit..It's really nice up here

Chris: The food is outstanding..I have it set up as buffet..It's only us anyway..So..Everybody can have whatever they want

Vic: I like that..Ladies..Have a seat..The ladies sit in one side of the table and the men on the other side

Marlon: Why guys?

Kim: I just prefer to be away from Chris..I know he is going to get up so many times

Chris: You better believe it..I love buffet

Marvin: Marlon and I wanted to have it..With waiters..The buffet was Chris idea

Chris: C'mon Marvin..You are throwing me under the bus as if I am the only one who loves buffet

Marlon: Guys don't be shy..This is for you..The whole floor is yours..Go ahead eat as much as you can..We have it early..At six..So everybody can have enough time to digest and get ready for tomorrow

Kourt: Before a big case..I can never eat..My appetite shut down

Chris: For me that's the opposite..Before a big case I pig out

Marvin: I don't think it's only before a big case

Ron: See Chris..What are you going to do with these guys?

Chris: I know..He is my brother though

Marlon: Guys..Everybody can prepare a small opening statement

Brianna: That's nice

Marlon: I know Brianna is dying to try her wings as a defense lawyer

Brianna: not only that..This case is kind of close to me..She is a friend..She is a woman..They want to make an example out of her

Renee: The prosecution is going to be prepared from what I heard

Malika: Definitely..We have to be ready to object and put up a real fight

Chris: It's going to be on

Marlon: Guys..Have you tried the shrimps?..They are delicious

Kim: What are they?

Chris: Shrimps Kim

Kim: What kind?

Renee: I tried them..They are coconut shrimps..They are very good

Chris: The drinks are on this side..Let me get the bottles of champagne

Malika: I really like the atmosphere..The music is nice..Perfect

Brianna: It is peaceful

Ron: I like the ambiance..Very quiet

Vic: How long you guys think the case will last?

Marlon: No more than three days..There are no witnesses

Vic: That's very true

Marlon: In a case like that..It is very important that you have a big team

Ron: Right..There are no witnesses..Every member on the team has a chance to make a statement and have an impact on the jury

Kourt: This is why the prosecution is certainly putting together a big team as well

Brianna: No doubt..I was told they have a team of eight

Marlon: That's big..When a D.A. put together a big team..They intend to win

Marvin: They don't stand a chance..We are not even complete yet..Olivier might join us

Kourt: The dream team baby

Brianna: Kourt..Pass me the champagne please

Kourt: If you drink you will not be ready for tomorrow

Brianna: C'mon Kourt

Kourt: Aren't Khlo doing the first opening statement?

Marlon: Yes..Are you ready Khlo?

Brianna: Always

_A couple hours later

Ron: Guys what time is it?

Marvin: It's eight fifteen

Chris: C'mon Ron..Don't tell me you are sleepy already

Ron: I like to get a good night sleep before a trial..At least a good seven hours

Vic: I agree with you Ron..I am the same way..Did you write something already Ron?

Marlon: C'mon Vic..You know him better than that..Ron does not write before a statement

Kourt: Really..You don't put anything on paper at all?

Ron: I like to talk form my heart

Brianna: I do that sometimes..But for tomorrow..I think I will write something

Malika: I always write my statements prior..I like to be prepared

Renee: Me too..I like to be ready..I feel more confident when my statement is written

Kim: Let me tell you guys what happen to me one time..I was going to pitch my business in Monaco..There were six major designers there in the room..I put my hand in my pocket and I realized that I changed jacket and left my speech in my other jacket

Brianna: What did you do Kim?..Oh my god..This is not a good situation to be in

Kim: Tell me about it

Renee: That happened to me once

Kourt: Really?

Chris: The ladies are too forgetful

Kim: Forgetful or not..I don't think they forget about the things you did to them

Chris: Oh my god Kim..I can never get a break..Can I?

Malika: Blame yourself for that Chris

Marvin: That's the price you pay for trying to be player of the year every year

Chris: Marv..Really brother?..On what team are you on?

Ron: We are one team here..Aren't we?

Vic: That's what I thought

Marlon: C'mon guys..We are one team..We must remain focus..Can't let you kill my brother Chris..We are going to need him..He is the bravest guy in court

Marvin: Not the bravest..He is the craziest..During the hearing..Did you hear what he told the judge?

Brianna: What did he tell the judge?

Chris: I am flattered..I did not think you would be interested to hear it Khlo?

Brianna: Just want to hear the craziness you did

Marlon: He told the judge to hold his horses

Ron: Really?

Vic: How he escaped jail after that?

Chris: I am not crazy..First..I told him with all due respect

Marlon: I think the judge realized that he was wrong for making a derogatory statement toward our client

Chris: That's why I went for his neck..I told him t hold his derogatory horses

Ron: Very funny

Brianna: That's disrespectful

Kourt: He should have locked you up Chris

Chris: Oh my god..Look at my haters

Renee: I don't think they hate you Chris..They love you too much

Chris: That's what it is..Well..This love is killing me

Marlon: Guys..I think it's time for us to leave..Everybody has to be ready for tomorrow

Brianna: Kim..Are you coming tomorrow?

Kim: Yes..I will be there early..I have to bring the dress for Marilyn..Makeup..My girl has to look good

Marlon: We appreciate all you are doing for our client Kim..We thank you

Kim: Don't thank me..This is a duty to me..She is like a sister to me..I owe her this

Brianna: Aw..She is so kind

Kourt: I wish someone could as kind as Kim is

Renee: Who are you talking about Kourt?

Brianna: Don't pay no mind to her..She is talking about me..Hating on me as usual

Kourt: Nobody is hating on you..I am just telling the truth

Brianna: Why are you the only one who thinks that I am mean?

Kourt: they probably think it but don't want to say it

Chris: I am with you on that Kourt

Malika: Chris..If I were you I would remain quiet

Chris: Whatever

_The day of the trial has arrived..The team members begin to arrive at the courthouse parking lot..Chris was the first to arrive..Then Marlon arrives..Ron..A few minutes later..Vic..Brianna..Malika..Khlo..Renee..Marvin..Kourt..By eight thirty five the defense team was complete and ready for battle..By eight forty five..The prosecution team arrives in a blue van and makes their way to the courtroom as if they were on a very important mission..Kim gets there at seven forty five..She brings a very nice dress for Marilyn..And she also brings one of her hair stylists with her to do Marilyn's hair..And makeup..Marilyn is looking great..Then Gary arrives..He is looking a little weak..But nevertheless he is here to support Marilyn..After all without his sacrifice..Marilyn could have been dead by now..Gary walks in..Goes to the defense table and shakes hand with all the members..Looks towards Marilyn and smiles..Extends his arms and grabs her hand..And whispers "Be Strong..I Am with You" Then goes and sits next to Kim..The courtroom's atmosphere a bit tense..The defense team members are not talking to each other..Nor are the prosecution team members..Very tense..You can feel it..It's the calm before the storm

-Guys..It's that time..Follow me..Let's go into the courtroom..We can't afford to miss this..A few minutes later a loud voice shatters the heavy silence:

Bailiff: All rise please..This court is now in session

Judge: Thank you..Have a seat please..Good morning everyone..We have a crowded courtroom here..Haven' we?..A large crowd is not necessary a bad thing..As long you follow the rules of my courtroom everything should go smoothly..But..If you don't follow the rules..I will be your worst nightmare..What is that young woman laughing about?..You seem to be pretty young..What are doing in the courtroom at this time?..Why aren't you in school?

Young Lady: I am a law student your honor

Judge: You are?

Young Lady: Yes your honor

Judge: First thing I want you to learn is..The courtroom is not a place for laughter..It is not a comedy club..Do you hear me?

Young Lady: Yes your honor

Judge: Now..I want you to leave..So you can remember in the future that a courtroom is far different from a comedy club..You would remember that?

Young Lady: I guess

Judge: I want to hear yes or no

Young Lady: Yes your honor

Judge: Ok..Now leave please..Let this be an example for all..My courtroom is not a place to play games..If anyone wants to play..Now is the time to leave..Because later there will be a price to pay when violates the rules..You will be charged with contempt to court..You will be thrown in jail..You don't want to go to jail..So..Respect the rules please..The gallery does not talk in my courtroom..The counselors talk if you have the floor..If you object..You must wait for my authorization..I come out as a mean judge..Not at all..You all have been in a courtroom before..You are all professional here..I am not a mean judge at all..I simply love discipline..I hope I made myself clear..If you have any question now is the time to ask

Marlon: Your honor..I have a motion

Judge: A motion?..We haven't even started yet?

Marlon: I am sorry your honor..Not a motion..I meant to say a request

Judge: You look familiar..What is your name?

Marlon: Marlon Hampton

Judge: You are one of the guys from M,M&C Firm

Marlon: Yes your honor

Judge: I see..I heard of you guys..The whole team is here today..No one is left at the office today?

Marlon: Pretty much the whole team is here your honor

Judge: I see..You guys are ready for battle?

Marlon: It's good to be ready

Judge: What is your request sir?

Marlon: Your honor..Considering the health condition of our client..She might need to leave the courtroom depending on how she feels

Judge: That should not be a problem at all..Young lady..Whenever you want to leave the courtroom..Just let me know

Marilyn: Thank you your honor

Judge: You should not worry about leaving the courtroom..You have an army here doing work on your behalf..Anymore questions..Requests..Let's hear it now

Marlon: No your honor..That's all for now

Judge: The prosecution has any question

Prosecutor: No your honor

Judge: Nothing for now..Nothing you can think of?

Prosecution: No your honor

Judge: I am trying to be fair here..Having said that..Both sides are ready?..Defense?

Khlo: We are ready your honor

Judge: I know you..Well..I saw you before..You used to be a prosecutor..Didn't you?

Khlo: Yes your honor

Judge: You don't like them..They don't treat you right?

Khlo: A little bit of both your honor

Judge: Really?

Khlo: I am only kidding your honor..I certainly enjoyed working there..They were all very kind to me..It is the time for me to move on and do something different

Judge: Time to go on the other side of the fence

Khlo: Yes..The fence that is..Your honor

Judge: Well..Don't expect them to be kind to you now

Khlo: I am aware of that and ready as well

Judge: Prosecution..Are you ready?..Beside missing a member

Prosecution: You can survive a runaway member

Khlo: Objection your honor

Judge: Excuse me..Go ahead..She is ready for battle

Khlo: Your honor..I did not run away..It was simply time for me to move on..And I did just that..I did not know they would still be crying over that

Judge: I agree with you..When it's time to move on there is nothing that can be done about it..I myself worked for the prosecution office after graduating from law school..Having said that..Is the prosecution ready?

Prosecutor: Yes your honor

Judge: Thank you..Hopefully the process will go smoothly and the jury will not have to be here for a long time..Defendant please stands up please..How do you plead?

Marilyn: Not guilty your honor

Judge: Defense..You have informed your client regarding the deference between pleading guilty and not guilty

Marvin: Yes your honor..We have

Judge: Thank you..Prosecution..Are you ready for your opening statement?

Prosecutor: Yes your honor

Judge: You may proceed

Prosecutor: Thank you your honor..Good morning ladies and gentlemen of the jury..We appreciate that you took valuable time from your busy schedule to be here and help us in this courtroom today..I must begin by pointing that this is not a case that can refer to the 1973 Woe vs. Wade..This is not a right to choose case..It's completely different..This is a case where the state is doing a remarkable job by simply preventing the growth of a fetus which will not survive because the mother is contaminated with a deadly disease..This is an attempt by the state to prevent promiscuous and drug addict women from bringing sick babies into this world

Khlo: Objection your honor

Judge: It is only an opening statement counselor

Khlo: Your honor..With all due respect..I know it is an opening statement..But that statement made by the prosecution is outrageous..As a woman..I took it very personally..Your honor..The prosecutor said and I quote "This is an attempt by the state to prevent promiscuous and drug addict women from bringing sick babies into this world"..Your honor..My lips can barely form those words..This is such a shame..In the year two thousand and sixteen..To hear someone makes such a statement is mind boggling..Not just that your honor..Our client has never done drugs nor being promiscuous..Such statement should not have been made when talking about our client

Judge: I understand counselor..Your point is well taken..Prosecutor..Please don't use any derogatory statement when referring to the defendant

Malika: Your honor..We are not asking for any favor by asking the prosecution to refrain from defaming our client..For the prosecution information..Our client got infected at her job..While helping sick people..While serving her community

Judge: I understand..I see the defense came with a group of tigers ready to pounce..Prosecutor..I hope you understand the point they are trying to make

Prosecutor: Yes your honor..I do understand it..I apologize to the defendant

Judge: Defendant..The prosecution offered you an apology for referring to you as a drug addict

And being promiscuous..Do you accept the apology?

Marilyn: Yes your honor

Judge: Thank you..Now..It's time for us to proceed..Because..Ladies and gentlemen we don't have the whole year for this case..Precede prosecutor

Prosecutor: Thank you your honor..We are used to Miss Khlo's aggression in the courtroom

Judge: I would not call it aggression..She has a job to do..That is to defend her client..You would have appreciated it if she was still on your side..Wouldn't you prosecutor?

Prosecutor: You can say so your honor

Judge: Proceed please

Prosecutor: Thank you your honor..What I am trying to say is the state has an ultimate duty to establish a precedent..In order to prevent such atrocity from happening in the future..The state is not by any mean trying to interfere in the women right to choose..This is way different from Roe vs. Wade..The state has a duty to discourage women who are infected by a deadly disease from getting pregnant and thus giving birth to sick babies..Who will suffer and die..This is the only reason why the state is requesting that the defendant ends her pregnancy..By refusing to do so..The state has every right to imprison the defendant for disobeying the law..I hope all the jury members would understand the position of the state..I know the jury members are very intelligent people of our society..Whom will stand with the state in order to prevent such atrocity from happening..That is to bring a sick baby into this world that will stand no chance to survive..This is why the prosecution is very confidant the jury will find the defendant guilty..We the people of this society will stand together..We need your help..The good people of the jury..In order to make it happen..We must set a strong precedent in order to prevent this atrocity from becoming an everyday occurrence..I am confident and my colleagues are as confident as well..That the fine people of this jury will do what it's right..That is to find the defendant guilty..Thank you your honor

Judge: Thank you sir..The defense may proceed at this time..Hold on..What is the time?..It is already eleven forty five..The time did fly..Didn't it?..This is what I am going to do..We will take our first break right now since it is almost twelve o'clock

Chris: It is just a small break your honor or lunch break?

Judge: Lunch break..It is almost twelve o'clock..The court will adjourn now and will reconvene at two o'clock..I think it's a good thing for the defense

Marlon: How so your honor?

Judge: That will give you guys time to get prepared

Marvin: Your honor..We are always ready

Judge: To be more ready..I am only kidding..I heard of you guys..I do what you are capable of..Enjoy your lunch and I will see everybody back here at two o'clock..Not at five past two..At two sharp please..Please remain seated until the jury leaves the room..Lady with yellow dress..Do you understand what remain seated means?..Good..You might find yourself sitting in a cell..Thank you

_The people in the gallery make their way out of the courtroom..Marilyn gets a hug from each of her lawyers..She has a chance to meet Vic..Ron..Renee..Marvin..Chris..Khlo and Malika..Kim exchanges a few words with Marilyn while the guards impatiently waiting to take her back to her cell..Two guards grab her by her arms..She whispers I love you to Gary..To which Gary replies..I love too babe..The guards spin her around to begin the walk..Marilyn is looking back while walking in an attempt to see Gary..Kim and her lawyers one more time..While doing so..She is asking herself how her life turns into such a nightmare..The guards walk her to her cell..Marilyn has tears streaming down her face..The guards remove her handcuffs..Put her inside the cell and lock the door..She begins to cry while thinking how happy she used to be as a child..Soon she hears a noise by the small bed..She looks and her dad is there..Let's listen:

Marilyn: Daddy?..You are here?

Marilyn's Dad: Yes baby..I am with you all the time..I want you to be brave..Knowing that you are never alone..I will be with you every step of the way

Marilyn: Daddy..How did you get in here..This is jail..People don't get in and leave as they please

Marilyn's Dad: I am not people..I am a spirit

Marilyn: You look so nice daddy..I am so happy you are here with me..You always come to me at the right time

Marilyn's Dad: I am here to dry your tears..Everything that you are going through right now..It will all be in the past one day very soon

Marilyn: I can't wait for that day daddy..That's how much pain my heart can take

Marilyn's Dad: Don't cry

Marilyn: I am sorry daddy

Guards: Ma'am..Are you ok?..Did I hear you talking?

Marilyn: No sir..I am fine

_Meanwhile outside the courthouse

Marvin: Let's find a place to eat something

Khlo: I am not in the mood to eat..I have to go to the gym guys and workout a little..I will be back

Renee: Khlo is ready for battle

Kim: That's so sad..Marilyn was crying when the guards took her back to the cell

Malika: It is a sad thing

Vic: Taking one's freedom is never a fun thing

Khlo: Where is Kourt?..I will be back

Chris: She went to get her bag from her car

Renee: We should wait for her

Marlon: Guys..Let's use the time efficiently..We only have two hours..Let's eat something

Chris: Follow me everyone..I know a place not too far from here

Ron: Are we driving?

Chris: No it's a walking distance

Kourt: Who is going to start the opening statement?

Marlon: I don't know..Any volunteer?

Marvin: I don't mind

Marlon: Let's get to the restaurant then we will decide..I think the best thing to do it's to let everyone say something

Kourt: That is if the judge will let us

Khlo: I think she will..She does not seem to be a mean judge at all..Guys I have to run

Ron: Don't let that fool you..I had a case..The judge was very jovial..One of my colleagues took it for granted and ended up being held in contempt

Malika: You are right..We must always be respectful

Marvin: Guys..Just don't be like Chris

Chris: Like Chris?..What did I do?

Marlon: Don't tell the judge to hold his horses

Vic: I don't think it's a good idea..I was held in contempt once..Don't tell me I am the only one?

Kourt: Khlo and I..We did not get held in contempt but we came close

Kim: Really?..When was that?

Kourt: It was during the good deed case..The judge had it with us

Renee: It was before they had fallen in love with each other

Kim: Really?

Kourt: She was hating on me big time..She enjoys a good fight..I had a good time myself..I remembered the judge told us..Next time both of you are going to jail

Vic: That's how you guys became best friends?

Kourt: Pretty much..I don't know about best friends..Not best friends..She is in love with me

Brianna: Really?..Don't talk behind my girl back like that

Kourt: This is why she is no longer a prosecutor

Marvin: Did not know it was the reason she quitted the job

_One hour and forty five minutes later

Marlon: Guys it is that time to go back..This is what we are going to do..We are going to let the ladies handle the opening statements

Chris: I agree..Where is Khlo?

Kourt: She had to go meet her trainer..She is at the gym

Ron: Are you guys sure she will be back on time?

Chris: If she is not back on time.,Just replace her..Not a big deal at all..Drop her from the case period

Marlon: The guys will close it

Marvin: Chris is fighting her even when she is not there

Chris: I think it's simply because I love too much..Right?

Kim: You are so right

Marlon: Do you agree ladies?..Khlo is back guys?

Chris: No she is not..We will proceed without her

Kourt: Perfect

Brianna: What did you think..I told you I was coming back..You guys need to trust me a little more

Chris: Well..You and your trainer are annoying

Brianna: You are jealous Chris?

Chris: Jealous?..Not at all..You play too damn much with that guy

Kourt: Chris..If only you knew where Brianna's heart is

Chris: Where is it?

Kourt: It's not you or the trainer..You are both out of the picture..Should I tell them Khlo

Brianna: Go ahead..You seem to know what is going on in my life more than everybody

Kourt: Yes I do

Marvin: Who is that lucky guy Brianna?

Brianna: Ask Kourt..She is the reporter

Renee: I know who he is..Frankly..I have not seen her so into a guy before..She adores that guy

Brianna: Oh my god..What is it?..My whole life story is being told in the streets..Really?

Renee: I am only saying what I heard from you..You said that you adore him..You love his work..You love what she stands for

Brianna: Enough already..Can we concentrate on the case?

Chris: Whatever that is that she loves so much..I think that trainer nonsense will get her in trouble

Brianna: Chris..Please..You don't know me..When I love someone..I try my best to please him..Therefore..There will be no trainer..No one for that matter will be able to jeopardize our love

Kourt: Wow..I love that..I am so proud of you..I know what I will do..When I see the guy that you love..I will say..The trainer did it again

Brianna: And I will smack you in your mouth Kourt

Kim: What do you think he would do..If Kourt does such a thing

Brianna: He loves me a lot..He does not want anybody to play those types of games when it comes to me..He does not like to get embarrassed..I don't think he would appreciate it much

Renee: You think it's enough for him to break up with you?

Brianna: No..But..I don't want to upset him..He is a very nice guy..Great humor..But..When he is upset he can say things you don't want to hear..Why get him mad..I love him guys..You guys don't know what love is..That's why

Kourt: Oh my god..Look who is talking

Brianna: Kourt..You are just hating..You are trying everything you can to get us apart

Kourt: You are so wrong..I like to bother you..But..I really like it when you are happy..I like to tease you..But that's about it..I love you like a sister

Brianna: Nice to hear from you..It means a lot to me

Chris: Ladies..Walk a little faster..You guys are way behind..We are getting late

Ron: Whatever they are talking about..Must be very interesting

Vic: I know..They are laughing and having a good time

Marvin: So guy..Is it a unified decision?..To let the ladies open..And the guys will close..Right?

Marlon: Yes..Guys..Do you all agree?

Renee: I don't see anything wrong with it..Who will start it?

Brianna: I will

Marlon: Great..Brianna will start..Let's go in there and handle business

_In the courtroom

Bailiff: All rise please..This court is now in session

Judge: Have a seat please..Everybody had a good lunch?..The prosecution did its opening statement before we left for lunch..Defense..Are you ready?

Marlon: Yes your honor..We are ready

Judge: The defense has the floor

Brianna: Thank you your honor..Good afternoon ladies and gentlemen of the jury..Today is a very special day for me..It is a very special day..Because since I was a little girl in school..I always stood up against bullying..Today is very special to me..Because once again I have the opportunity to stand against bullying..I am so glad that you the people of this jury joined me in accomplishing this task..They often say..Those who stand by and do nothing..Watch one being abused and taking advantage of is as guilty as the actual offender..So..This is our opportunity to intervene..We must intervene in order to prevent such thing from happening in our life time..As I stand before you this afternoon..My blood is boiling in my veins..My blood is boiling in my veins simply because..Here we have an innocent young woman..Thrown in prison simply because she refused to have an abortion..Simply because she refused to end the life of her unborn child..She is thrown in prison simply because she wants to keep the greatest gifts that god gave her..She is only doing what has been done for many centuries..She is trying to do something that is even written in the bible..That is to multiply..And bring more gods' children on this planet..Today she is the unlucky one..She is single out and chosen to be the first victim of the state..I am begging you to excuse my emotion..As a woman myself..This case is very personal to me..Here we have nine women in our jury..This could have been any of you..We also have three men in the jury..This could have been your daughter..Your sister..Any female member of your family..Now is the time for us to stand as one..Now is the time..To send a loud and clear message to the state..The message is..We will not be pushed around by some politicians..We will not be pushed around by those working for the lobbyists in Washington..We are here as one..We are here to prevent such injustice from happening in the United States of America..This is the very reason we gather here today..This is a very important gathering..This is a gathering that will leave its prints and path for our children and grand children..This gathering in this courtroom is simply to say..Never again should our civil liberty and woman right to choose should be taking for granted..Never again should they be on by any state..I am confident..That together we will accomplish that task..Too often our kindness is taking for granted..We are here to say enough is enough..I am confident that at the end of this trial..Our client will be found not guilty..You heard the prosecution mentioned in their opening statement..That the state is simply trying to prevent the suffering of a child..A child whom will be doomed..I am here to tell you..That the state is completely wrong..Based on surveys done..Surveys based on years of studies..The number of children who are born infected with the disease is very low..Therefore..That theory that the state is trying to push into our head will not fly..We will not let them kill our client's baby before he or she could even have a chance at life..This unborn child could be the very person that will find a cure for the disease..We cannot afford to let that happen..I am sorry for the tears in my eyes..I am sorry..This case is very personal to me..This is outrageous to think that they want to kill her baby just to make some political point..To create a precedent..This is unacceptable..Therefore..We must stand together to say no to such injustice..And we must let it be known..That such injustice will not take place in this courtroom..Today..Ladies and gentlemen of the jury..You have an ultimate task..Not often one has such opportunity..Today..You have the opportunity to make history..You have the opportunity to carve a path through the stony mountain of everyday politics..A path of justice on which our children and grand children would walk peacefully..A path on which they can walk and one day become parents..A path on which..You the people of the jury set the first stone..The only way to do so..It is to find our client not guilty..This is the only way to send a clear message to the politicians..So our client can be released and go home..Where she can take care of herself and her unborn child..Whom someday can maybe be the one who finds the cure for the disease..Thank you your honor

Judge: Thank you counselor..Very eloquent

Brianna: Thank you your honor..I apologize for my emotion

Judge: You are human..It is understandable..If a case is close to your heart..It is only natural that emotions surface..Regardless of emotions..I think you did a great job..It reminded me of the days when I was a defense lawyer..As a woman myself..It is always a pleasure to see women display that level of eloquence on the floor

Brianna: Thank you your honor..At this time your honor I would like to yield the floor to my colleague Renee

Judge: Proceed please

Renee: Thank you your honor..Good morning ladies and gentlemen of the jury..Your honor..I am not making an opening statement..Your honor..The defense has a motion

Judge: What is the motion about?

Renee: Your honor..The motion is about the annulment of the trial

Judge: To motion for the annulment of the trial..You will need valid argument..What is your argument?

Renee: Your honor the defense believes that our client rights were violated by the state

Judge: What rights are we talking about counselor?

Renee: Your honor..Her human right..Her civil right..Her civil liberty..Her right to choose..Your honor..I deeply believe..This might be the only opportunity we have in order to create a strong precedent

Judge: I must remind you that the state only holds your client because it has taken possession of the unborn child

Renee: Your honor..That in itself is unconstitutional..The constitution does not warrant such action your honor..To throw a pregnant woman in prison on the pretence of taking possession of the baby is wrong in every sense..Not only lawfully wrong your honor..Morally wrong..And it is against every humanitarian rule..Therefore your honor..We are asking the court to do what is necessary..That is to end the trial and release our client to her family..That's the only right thing to do your honor..I am calling not only on your knowledge of the law of the land but also in your kind heart..As a woman yourself your honor..I know that our client's situation must have affected you..She is a young lady who recently lost her dad to cancer..Her mother is currently battling cancer..She is dealing with a very serious health issue herself..Then come the state trying to rip her baby from her belly..As if what she is going through is not enough..Your honor..I am asking you today to annul the trial and release our client to her family..We cannot sit around and let the state make an example out of her..She is just another innocent young woman..She needs some mercy your honor and the protection granted by the law..Thank you

Judge: Thank you counselor..As you may know counselor..This is a very delicate situation..This is a very unusual case..Therefore..The decision to annul the trial will not come easy..Since..It is already three forty five..I will inform the court of my decision tomorrow morning..At this time..The court will adjourn until tomorrow..Thank you..Please remain seated until the jury walks out..Have a good night

_The next day

Bailiff: The court is now in session

Judge: Have a seat everyone..Everybody had a good night of sleep..I did not sleep well last night..Somehow..I was tormented by the decision I had to make regarding the case..That is regarding the annulment of the case..I really feel and understand what the defendant is going through..I am a mother myself..I know how much it means to her to keep her baby..But..I have to push my feelings to the side..And do what the law requires to be done in this situation..Because this case has no precedent..If only that case had precedent..It would have been much more easier to decide..I am torn..But..I had to make a decision..And I have decided that the case will go on..The defense has a strong team..A team of very qualified lawyers..Therefore..The defendant stands a good chance to fight a good fight and be found not guilty..Having said that..My decision is final and we will proceed with the trial

_Whispers at the defense table

Renee: I think we should challenge the judge decision

Brianna: Go for it..What do you think Marlon?

Marlon: Go for it

Renee: Your honor..With all due respect..I object to your decision..Your honor..This is our chance to do what is right..We cannot rely on the outcome of the case..Now is the time..This very minute is the time to do the right thing your honor..We might never have opportunity..Your honor..You do have the authority to end the trial right now..This case stands against everything we stand for as human beings your honor..Therefore your honor..I believe the extraordinary must be done in order to bring relief to that young woman..It must be done your honor I order to say no to this blatant disregard of human right..The defense is still confident your honor that somehow you will find it deep within your heart and bring solace to a young woman who so desperately needs it your honor..Your honor..Once again..It is with the greatest humility and respect that I am asking you this favor for our client..Your honor..We must show humility sometimes even in situation where strength would make us look better..We must try to sometimes make it easy for others..Your honor..Controlling strength and make way for humility and patience is a great sign of courage and self control..Therefore your honor..I am calling on your humility and your compassion in order to revisit your decision and annul the trial..It would send a strong message to the state..That in the year two thousand sixteen..This is no time to let such atrocity triumph in our courtrooms..I do appreciate your patience your honor..And once again..My objection was not by any mean a challenge of the authority you have in the courtroom..Thank you your honor

Judge: Well..Well..Well..Just when I thought this case would be a very short case..Here come more tigers unleashing claws..I knew that my courtroom could become a battlefield..From the size of the defense team..I just did not think the battle would become so soon..Yet..Against my decision..I don't take offense at all to the counselor objecting to my decision..I am one of those few judges who encourage vigorous defense when it comes to an attorney defending the rights of his or her client..But..Even though I am lenient..But..I must remain firm in this situation..Simply because my decision cannot be based solely on compassion..Our judicial records don't offer any precedent to this case..This is what makes it an exceptional case..I am just like everyone else human..I do understand what your client is going through at this time..But my hands are tied..Having said that..I do not expect my decision to be contested for a second time..My leniency sure does have its limits..I hope everyone..Especially the defense lawyers understand it..Therefore..My decision is to not annul the trial..We will proceed as scheduled..Having said that..It is already eleven thirty..We will now take our lunch break..The court will now adjourn and will reconvene at two o'clock..When we come back the prosecution will call its first witness..Please remain seated until the jury leaves the room..Have a good lunch..Don't be late please..Two o'clock..Not five minutes after

Renee: You heard that Chris

Chris: Me..Why me?

Judge: Who's Chris?

Chris: That's me your honor

Judge: Don't be late..He does not look like a guy with a habit of being late..He looks so sharp

Chris: Thank you your honor..Your honor..I get no love from the ladies

Judge: Well Chris..I refuse to believe that..They probably love you too much

Chris: You think so your honor

Judge: I do

Chris: Their loves are killing me your honor

Judge: You will survive..Have a great lunch everyone..Be here on time Chris

Chris: Definitely your honor

_In the parking lot

Chris: Brianna..You owe me one

Brianna: What?..What did you say?

Chris: You heard me

Renee: Chris..It was not Brianna

Chris: Who told the judge that I am always late?

Renee: It was me Chris..You know we love you..You are our only Chris

Marvin: Guys..Who is the witness the prosecution will introduce?

Ron: I believe he is a doctor..Right?

Marlon: Yes he is

Kourt: Where is Kim guys?

Renee: She went to the jail to have lunch with Marilyn

Vic: That's very kind of her

_An hour and thirty five minutes later

Bailiff: This court is now in session

Judge: Good afternoon everyone..Now is the time for the prosecution to introduce the first witness..Prosecution..Are you guys ready to call the first witness?

Prosecution: Yes your honor..The prosecution wants to call Dr. William Cohen

Bailiff: Please state your name for the court

Witness: William..Dr. William Cohen

Bailiff: Raise your right hand and repeat after me..I swear to tell the truth..Nothing but the truth

Witness: I swear to tell the truth..Nothing but the truth

Judge: Have a seat please sir

Witness: Thank you your honor

Prosecutor: Good afternoon doctor Cohen

Witness: Good afternoon

Prosecutor: We thank you doctor for taking very precious time from you're your schedule to be here this afternoon..Time you could have used to save lives..Time you could have used to help your community

Brianna: Objection

Judge: Sustained

Brianna: Your honor..We sure don't have all year as you have mentioned at the beginning of the trial..It seems that the whole year will go by while he is making love to the witness

Prosecutor: Your honor..This is not love making at all..I am simply thanking Doctor Cohen for being here..That woman is acting out of control here

Kourt: Your honor if you allow me..I am not going to sit here and let mister prosecution address my colleague in that manner..He is so used to degrade women..This is why he is talking in that manner to my colleague

Prosecutor: Your honor..I only said that she is out of control

Brianna: Colbert..Don't make me start with you..You know better

Prosecutor: Start what?..Take your best shot Brianna

Judge: Order please..Order in my courtroom..This is not the WWF royal rumble..This is a courtroom..My courtroom..Please..It will be respected or a lot of you will be spending the night in a cell..I don't want any exchange of words between the two parties..Did I make myself clear?..Order please..Prosecutor you may proceed

Prosecutor: Thank you your honor..Doctor Cohen..Once again thank you for being here..I did not know a simple thank you would certain people erupt

Judge: Prosecutor..Proceed with the questioning of the witness please

Prosecutor: Yes your honor..Doctor Cohen..How long have you been a doctor sir?

Witness: For fifteen years sir

Prosecutor: What kind of doctor are you sir..Let me rephrase that..What is your expertise sir

Witness: I am a general practitioner

Prosecutor: Thank you sir..You are also an expert in contagious illnesses..Are you not?

Witness: Not an expert..But I did some studies in that field

Prosecutor: Doctor..You know what this case is about..Do you not?

Witness: Yes sir

Prosecutor: The defendant refused to have an abortion..She is infected with a deadly disease..Don't you think it's a very cruel decision?

Brianna: Objection your honor..The witness is not here to judge the decision of our client..He is a medical doctor..He is not a specialist in human behavior..Our client is an adult..She what she pleases regarding her health..That's her body..Whether the prosecutor or witness thinks it is cruel..It's only a matter of opinion..The witness is not here to pass judgment

Judge: The defense has a point here..The witness is a medical doctor..Keep the questions within the medical realm..Proceed please

Prosecutor: Thank you your honor..Doctor Cohen..Based on the studies that you have made..The baby has a chance to be born infected with the disease..Does he not sir?

Witness: Yes..The baby stands a chance to be born infected with the virus

Prosecutor: Therefore doctor..It is best to remove the baby in order to prevent that from happening..Isn't it doctor?

Renee: Objection your honor

Judge: Sustained

Renee: Your honor the witness does not know what is best for our client

Judge: Counselor..Reformulate your question please

Prosecutor: Doctor Cohen..Leaving the baby in the defendant stomach will put the baby at risk..Will it not sir?

Witness: The chance for the baby to survive after birth is very minimal..Isn't it doctor?

Prosecutor: Doctor Cohen..In such situation what would you recommend?

Kourt: Objection your honor

Judge: Sustained

Kourt: Your honor..The witness is not here to make recommendations..The decision of the case is only depend on the people of the jury..It's an attempt to influence the jury your honor

Judge: Prosecutor..You heard the defense..The decision in the case should be left to the jury

Prosecutor: Doctor Cohen..You can say that the baby is at risk..Can you not?

Witness: Yes sir

Prosecutor: No further questions your honor

Judge: The defense may now cross examine the witness

Brianna: Thank you your honor..Good afternoon Sir

Witness: Good afternoon

Brianna: Sir..You are not an expert in contagious illnesses..Are you sir?

Witness: I did some studies

Brianna: Sir..You did not answer my question..Are you an expert..Yes or no?

Witness: No I am not

Brianna: Thank you..It was a simple question..Was it not..You are a doctor..Right?

Prosecutor: Objection

Judge: Sustained

Prosecutor: Your honor the counselor is using sarcasm during the questioning of the witness

Brianna: What sarcasm?..I only told him..It was a pretty easy question..I think the suit you are wearing today is made by sensitivity..Just go up there and have him seated on your lap

Prosecutor: You heard that your honor

Judge: Order please..No exchange please..Or you will be held in contempt..Proceed counselor

Brianna: Thank you your honor..Doctor Cohen..Did I pronounce your name right sir?

Witness: Yes..Cohen

Brianna: I just don't want to upset the prosecutor

Judge: Counselor..Stay within what is relevant to the case

Brianna: Doctor Cohen..I heard you mentioned during the questioning..That it would be cruel for our client to carry the baby for a full term..My question to you doctor is..Don't you think this baby deserve a chance to become a responsible member of our society?

Prosecutor: Objection

Judge: Overruled..The witness can answer the question

Witness: Well..I think every baby deserves a chance to become a responsible member of our society..But this case is very different

Brianna: What make it so different doctor?

Witness: The mother is infected with a deadly disease

Brianna: Doctor..Do you know that the number of babies who died from an infected mother is very minimal?

Witness: Well

Brianna: Sir..Well is not the answer to the question..You stated that you are not an expert..Did you not?

Witness: I am not

Brianna: I should not expect you to know that the number of baby's death is minimal..Dr Cohen..Do you have Children sir?

Prosecutor: Objection

Judge: Sustained

Prosecutor: Your honor..The defense is asking irrelevant questions to the witness

Judge: The witness may answer the question

Witness: Yes..I do have children

Brianna: Doctor Cohen..My question to you is sir..Would you like your daughter to be treated as such sir?

Witness: Well..If she is

Brianna: Yes or no sir

Witness: I would not like my daughter to be in such situation

Brianna: Doctor Cohen..If you would not like your daughter to be in such situation..Why are you entertained by our client's situation?

Prosecutor: Objection

Judge: Overruled..The witness can answer the question

Witness: I am not at all entertained..I am simply giving my professional opinion regarding the matter

Brianna: But doctor..You said that you not an expert..Did you not?

Witness: Yes I did

Brianna: Therefore doctor Cohen..That would make your opinion irrelevant..Would it not?

Witness: Well

Brianna: Yes or no sir?

Witness: Yes

Brianna: No further questions your honor

Judge: Thank you..The prosecution may now redirect if it wishes to do so

Prosecutor: Thank you your honor..Doctor Cohen..The court understands that you are not an expert in contagious illnesses..But..You did work for many years in that field..Did you not?

Witness: Yes sir

Prosecutor: For how many years to be exact doctor?

Witness: Ten years

Prosecutor: No further questions your honor

Judge: Thank you..I chose to have the prosecution doing a redirect after each cross examination..Just because the defense has so many lawyers..I wanted to give the prosecution a chance to address each cross examination..Is that fair?

Marlon: The defense has no problem with that your honor

Judge: Thank you..I appreciate your understanding..Having said that..The defense may proceed with the cross examination

Kourt: Thank you your honor..Dr. Cohen..How are you today sir?

Witness: I am fine thank you

Kourt: Sir..From what I understand..It is your recommendation for our client to have an abortion..Isn't it sir?

Witness: Yes ma'am

Kourt: Doctor..You suggested that the state should have the right to kill our client's baby..Did you not sir?

Prosecution: Objection

Judge: Overruled..The witness may answer the question

Kourt: Killing our client's baby..Is your recommendation..Isn't it sir?

Witness: Well

Kourt: Yes or no sir?

Witness: Well..In the context

Kourt: Sir..Are you going to answer the question or you are going to play around it..And kill time..Since killing seems to be your expertise..Yes or no sir?

Prosecutor: Objection

Judge: Sustained

Prosecutor: Your honor..Doctor Cohen is not the one on trial here..He is here simply as a good Samaritan to the court..It seems that the defense wants to make him pay for their client

Judge: The question is pretty simple..The witness should answer the question

Kourt: You suggested that the state should be able to kill our client's baby..Did you not sir?

Witness: yes

Kourt: Doctor Cohen..Like every doctor..You took an oath to save lives..Did you not sir?

Witness: Yes

Prosecutor: Objection

Judge: Sustained

Prosecutor: Your honor..The defense is asking questions that have no relevancy to the case

Judge: Defense may proceed

Kourt: Doctor..You did take an oath to save lives..Didn't you sir?

Witness: Yes

Kourt: Doctor..Recommending the killing of our client's baby is not in compliance with the oath..Is it Doctor?

Witness: I would say

Kourt: Yes or no doctor

Witness: No

Kourt: Therefore Doctor..By recommending the killing of our client's baby..You are in effect doing something which does not meet the moral standard of a doctor..Are you not?

Witness: I simply wanted to give my opinion on the matter

Kourt: Sir..You admitted that your opinion does not matter during the redirect of my colleague..The court no longer cares about your opinion on this matter sir..The question is..Recommending the killing of our client's baby does not meet the moral standard of a doctor..Does it sir?

Witness: No

Kourt: No further questions your honor

Judge: Thank you..The prosecution may now redirect

Prosecutor: The prosecution will rest your honor

Judge: Does the defense want to further cross examine the witness?

Chris: No your honor..The defense would like to call its first witness..If you allow it your honor

Judge: I don't see any problem with hat..Let's give Doctor Cohen a chance to leave the stand and we will do so

Chris: Thank you your honor

Judge: Doctor Cohen..You may leave the stand sir..We thank you for your help

Witness: You are welcome

Judge: The defense may call its witness if it wishes to do so

Marvin: Thank you your honor

Brianna: Your honor..The defense will now called Kim Kroumani to the stand

Bailiff: State your name for the court please

Kim: Kim..Kim Kroumani

Bailiff: Please raise your right hand and repeat after me..I swear to tell the truth..Nothing but the truth

Kim: I swear to tell the truth..Nothing but the truth

Judge: Thank you..Have a seat please ma'am

Brianna: Good afternoon Miss Kroumani..How are you today?

Kim: I am fine thank you

Brianna: Miss Kroumani..You are friend with the defendant..Are you not?

Kim: Yes I am

Brianna: May I ask you what you do for living

Kim: I work in the fashion industry..I have my own modeling agency

Brianna: You must have a busy schedule..Don't you?

Kim: Yes..We are very busy..Our girls are in demand..Especially this time of the year

Brianna: We do appreciate that you take time from your busy schedule to be here..How long you and the defendant have been friends

Kim: I have known her for sixteen years..She is one of my best friends

Brianna: Miss Kroumani..The prosecution mentioned at the beginning of the trial that our client must be doing drugs..The prosecution suggested that this is why she got infected..Would you support such allegation?

Kim: Not at all..Not in this lifetime..Marilyn is the best human being I have ever known..She does not smoke or drink..Let alone to be called a drug addict

Brianna: I see that you have tears in your eyes..Why is that?

Kim: Because..I am sorry

Brianna: Take your time

Judge: Pass the box of tissue to her for me please..Remember ma'am..You may stop any time if you feel that you are getting overwhelmed by emotions

Kim: Thank you

Brianna: Tell the court why you are crying today

Kim: I know her for years many years..She is like a sister to me..To witness what she has gone through for the last two years..It's so sad..She lost her dad to cancer..Her mother is fighting for her life against cancer..Then..She got infected at her job..On top of that she is thrown in prison..This is not enough..They are trying to kill her baby..She does not deserve that

Brianna: Take your time..I am sorry about that

Judge: Do you want to continue ma'am

Kim: Yes..I am sorry about the tears..I just want to be there for her..She is my sister..I don't think she deserves that at all

Brianna: Why do you want to testify on her behalf today?

Kim: I just want the court to know that she deserves a better chance..She should not be forced to remove her baby

Brianna: Do you believe that her baby could become the one person who comes up with the cure for the disease?

Kim: I certainly believe so..Anything is possible

Brianna: No further question your honor

Judge: Thank you..The prosecution may cross examine the witness if it wishes to do so

Prosecutor: Your honor..The prosecution will rest

Judge: Does the defense have any more questions for Miss Kroumani?

Marvin: No your honor

Judge: Any motions please?

Marlon: No your honor

Prosecutor: No your honor

Judge: Thank you..At this time we are about ready to hand the case to the jury for deliberation..The court will adjourn for today and will reconvene tomorrow..Tomorrow morning..It will be closing arguments..Tomorrow..The session will start at ten o'clock..I hope everyone will appreciate the extra hour to get ready..I see some of you laughing..An hour can save your life when it comes to getting ready..Having said that..The session is now over..Please remain seated until the jury leaves the room..Have a good night everybody

_The next morning..Everybody is there early at the court house..There is very little talking..The anxiety is very thick..Then it is five minutes to ten..The courtroom is more crowded than usual..Let's go in..We cannot afford to miss this

Bailiff: All rise..This court is now in session

Judge: Have a seat please..Good morning everybody..As I told you yesterday..Today is closing arguments..Then it will be that time to hand the case to the jury..Having said that..Both parties are ready?

Prosecutor: Yes your honor

Marlon: Yes your honor

Judge: Prosecutor..You have the floor whenever you are ready

Prosecutor: Thank you your honor..Good morning ladies and gentlemen of the jury..I want to thank you for coming along with us into that journey..I also want to thank you particularly for taking time from your busy schedule to help us find a solution to this problem..A solution which the state needed to set an example..The right example..As you may know the state is simply concerned about our children's lives..Therefore..It has taken measures..And has decided to take possession of the unborn child..I want to bring to your attention that this case is not about the defendant..The state has absolutely no interest at all in keeping the defendant in jail..But..Since the defendant and the baby cannot be separated..The state has absolutely no choice but to keep the mother as well..That is the in this case the defendant..If the defendant is found guilty..The state will have the right to terminate the pregnancy..And thus preventing the suffering of the baby..You heard the testimony of doctor Cohen..He indicated that it is best for the mother to have an abortion..Because the baby stands no chance to survive..This is only why we gather here today..This is only why we call for your help today..We are only trying to do what is right..And the only way for this to be done..It is for you the good people of the jury to find the defendant guilty..By doing so..You will set an example..That will forever..You will set a needed precedent..You will send a clear and loud message to the women out there that are using drugs and get infected..And it will not be tolerated to bring a sick baby on this planet

Brianna: Objection

Judge: Overruled..This is a closing statement..There will be no debate counselor..You can respond at the time of your closing statement when you have the floor

Brianna: Your honor I simply wanted to mention that our client is not a drug addict..I don't want the prosecutor to poison the jury members' mind with such statement

Judge: I guess you mentioned what you wanted

Brianna: Thank you your honor

Judge: You are welcome..No more objections please..Prosecution may proceed

Prosecutor: Thank you your honor..We are deeply relying on you today to do what is right..And we are confident that the defendant will be found guilty..And the state will be granted the right to end her pregnancy..I know you heard the testimony of the defendant's friend..That should not affect you..They don't understand the example the state is trying to set..This is why..The prosecution is confident to hand the case to you the good people of this jury..And rest assured that justice will be done and the defendant will be found guilty..Thank you your honor

Judge: Thank you counselor..The defense may now do its closing statement..Defense..Are you ready

Ron: Yes your honor..We are ready

Judge: Proceed please

Ron: Good afternoon ladies and gentlemen of the jury..It is with a heart full of chagrin that I must stand before you this morning..And try to say a word or two..And hope those words will help save the life of our client's baby..This should not have been the situation today..This gathering should not have been for such reason..Considering the many years of suffering that those before us had gone through..Considering the work they have done to build and pave a pathway..A pathway to peace..A pathway to freedom..A pathway to justice..Yet today ladies and gentlemen..We gather in this room trying to prevent the destruction of that pathway..My heart is filled with chagrin due the enthusiasm of the prosecution to kill our client's baby..My heart is filled with chagrin due to the testimony of Doctor Cohen..A man whom took an oath to save lives..Yet..Walked in this room with the intention to kill our client's baby..My heart is filled with chagrin but yet my soul is rejoicing..My soul is rejoicing knowing that the good people of this jury will not let such injustice happen in this courtroom..My heart is rejoicing knowing not everyone shares the views and opinions of the prosecution and the state..As I stand before you today..I stand with the belief that justice will be found..I stand with the belief that the evil thoughts and intention of the prosecutor will not prevail..I stand here and still have a strong faith in the American justice system..A system which was put together to protect the people of this nation..Today my dear friends..I am humbly standing before you to ask you for a second chance for our client..I am humbly asking you to say no to the evil power of the state..I am confident that the people of this jury will find our client innocent..This judgment will not only be beneficial to our client..It will be a token which will guarantee that injustice can no longer be tolerated in our society..It will be an award to those who have been bullied for years..This judgment will be the first drop of rain which will cause the flood that will drown injustice in every crevice of our society..I stand before you today..With my soul pregnant with the hope that justice will be triumphant..Too often we stand around and let those sitting behind a desk in Washington do as they pleased..Now is the time..When we must all stand up as one..Now is the time to say enough is enough..Now is the time for us to break the silence..Now is the time for us to stand and say that we will no longer take part in the conspiracy..Now is the time..When we all must stand together and say no to fabrications and bullying..Ladies and gentlemen..It is a shame..That so long..So long..We have been the puppets of this bullying system..Today..You are asked to participate in the killing of our client's baby..Tomorrow it will be the killing of your own babies..Therefore..This courtroom is no place to let the state get away with such atrocity..This courtroom is no place to let injustice prevail..Our client is a decent young lady..Just like the prosecutor's daughter..She needs the respect and protection of the justice system..Just like any human being her human rights should be respected..I understand that the prosecution would like to win one more case..I understand that the prosecution would like to win one more trophy..But..Today is not the day..This courtroom is not the place..And this jury will make sure it does not happen..This jury will make sure that our client's human right is protected..This jury will make sure that our client's civil liberty is protected..This jury will make sure that the life of our client's baby is protected..This jury will make sure that our client's baby grows up and becomes a valuable member of our society..We are sorry..But we have no choice but to say "Not today" to the prosecution..We have no choice but to say "Not in this court room" to the prosecution..As we hand the case to the jury..We will rest assured that justice will be served..We will rest assured that there will never be another case where the state becomes the executor of our unborn babies..As we get ready to hand the case to the good people of this jury..We are confident that the result will be a reflection..An affirmation if you will..That the work of many good people who gave their lives fighting against injustice was not in vain..In order for that to happen..You must find our client not guilty..This is the only way that you will send a clear message to the state..That there is no room for that kind of injustice in our society..This is the only way to let the prosecution and the state know that today is a new day..It is to find our client not guilty..Thank you your honor

Judge: Thank you counselor..I am not disappointed at all..Very eloquent..This is not for no reason everyone is talking about the talent of the guys at M,M&C Law Firm

Marlon: Thank you your honor..It is a team effort

Judge: At this time..The case will be handed to the jury for deliberation..The court will adjourn..And will reconvene when a verdict is reached..I am asking everyone to remain in the vicinity of the court..Just in case a verdict is reached..So..We don't have to wait for someone to fly in from France or Italy..You guys are laughing..But it happened..We reached a verdict once and one of the attorneys was in the Bahamas..We don't want that..At least I don't want that..If that happens..Somebody will held in contempt to court..Understood?..Thank you..Having said that..Now is the last chance if any of the parties has a motion..Speak up now..I guess it's a no motion..Great..That means we can move on..We might reach a verdict this afternoon..At least..We hope..Having said that..Stay close by..Leave your contact number available please..Thank you..Please just remain seated until the jury leaves the room please..Thank you

_Outside in the parking lot

Marvin: Congrats Ron

Brianna: Congratulations..Very nice Ron

Vic: C'mon guys..Ron is the man..You already know

Marlon: It was a very good one..I am not surprised at all..You saw the work he did in redeemed

Kourt: I know..What are we doing?..Are we going to restaurant?

Marlon: Let's go get something to eat..Where is my man Chris?

Vic: Chris is still inside

Marvin: What is he doing inside still?

Kourt: He was talking to one of the prosecution ladies

Renee: The girl with the black hair?

Kourt: Yes

Brianna: He is coming

Chris: Sorry guys..I was exchanging info with a lady

Marvin: Always securing the phone number

Chris: No..No.Just business

Vic: Exactly..Can a man conduct business in peace?

Chris: I know right..Where are we going?

Marlon: We are going right across the street

Chris: C'mon guys..You guys know I am the man when it comes to nice places

Brianna: This is not a party Chris..We are waiting for a verdict

Chris: Oh my god..I never said it was a party

Brianna: You go back in the courtroom drunk if you want to

Marlon: Chris knows better

Chris: Right..One time I had a beer and the judge smell the beer..She said who has been drinking

Marlon: I know..It was a close one

Chris: At that point I was afraid to breathe..I learned my lesson

_An hour later while inside the restaurant Marlon's phone rang..Let's listen

Marlon: Hello..Yes this is Marlon

Court Clerk: Good afternoon..I am calling you sir to let you know the jury reached a verdict

Marlon: Thank you very much..We will be there

Marvin: What is happening..Hung jury?

Marlon: Nope..Put down your forks guys..We have to run..The jury reached a verdict

Brianna: Really..That was fast

Renee: I expected that

Kourt: Me too

Renee: An early verdict could mean a good thing

Vic: That's what they say..You can never be too optimistic when it comes to verdict

Ron: You are absolutely correct..We just have to go and see

Marlon: Ok guys..Let's get going..Ladies..Are you ready?

Brianna: Yes we are

_ Fifteen minutes later..Inside the courtroom for the reading of the verdict

Bailiff: All rise..This court is now in session

Judge: Thank you..Have a seat everyone..As I predicted..The verdict comes early..It is a very good thing for the jury..They will be able to be with their families and resume their regular schedules..Thank you all for your service..Having said that..We are not going to kill time..I think we should go straight to the reading of the verdict..Following the reading of the verdict..Regardless of the outcome..I don't want any cheering..Screaming..No expressing emotions in my courtroom..I saw a few of you already have tears in your eyes..Please..Control your emotions..It is a trial..If the outcome is not what you expected..Think of a basis for an appeal..Having said that..Who is the jury foreman?

Foreman: Me your honor

Judge: Foreman..Do you have a verdict?

Foreman: Yes your honor

Judge: May I have a copy of the verdict please?

Foreman: Yes you may your honor

Brianna: Your honor..Our client does not seem too well..Can the foreman hold on for a minute please?

Judge: Go ahead

Kim: Lyn..Lyn..Are you ok?

Kourt: Put some water on her face

Judge: Does she need medical attention?..Should we call an ambulance for her?

Brianna: Lyn..Lyn open your eyes baby

Malika: Lyn..Can you hear me?..Can you hear me?

Judge: Should we call an ambulance?

Marilyn: What happened?..What happened?

Kim: You fainted..Are you ok?

Marilyn: Did they read the verdict?..I am going to prison right?..They will kill my baby..Right?

Brianna: Not yet..Not yet..They haven't read the verdict yet

Judge: Is she going to be ok..Young lady..Can you hear me?

Marilyn: Yes..Yes your honor

Judge: Do you want some water?

Marilyn: Yes please

Kourt: I have a bottle of water right here

Judge: You came in my courtroom with water?

Kourt: It was in my bag your honor

Judge: You get a pass this time

Kourt: Thank you your honor

Judge: Do you want to leave the room..Or do you want to go and lay down

Marilyn: I am fine

Brianna: She said..She is fine your honor

Judge: She does not want to go back in the cell..I don't blame her

Brianna: Especially..Not if she does not have to go

Judge: I think she got overcome by emotions..Fear and the anxiety of waiting for the verdict can do that to you..I have seen it many times..I saw grown men collapsed before the reading of a verdict..Ok..I think..We should proceed..I would ask her to stand..I will make an exception..Can you stand young lady for the reading of the verdict?

Brianna: She said yes your honor

Judge: Foreman..Proceed please

Foreman: We the jury find the defendant Miss Marilyn April not guilty

Judge: The decision of the court is final..The defendant is to be released immediately to her attorneys

Marlon: Thank you your honor

Judge: You are welcome

Mindy: Lyn..Lyn..Are you ok?..Your dad is outside waiting for you..You are going to be late for class

Marilyn: Mom..Mom..Oh my god..I had such a bad dream..I dreamed that I got infected with HIV at a job..Then I became pregnant and got arrested

Mindy: I heard you making a noise..This is why I called you

Marilyn: It was such a bad dream mom..The state wanted me to have an abortion

Colbert: What is taking you guys so long?

Marilyn: Dad..Dad..I had a bad dream..I was in jail..And in trial for being pregnant..Dad you died of cancer in the dream..And mom had cancer

Mindy: That's a nightmare..You did not have the baby in the dream..Did you?

Marilyn: No

Mindy: I can't wait to hear the second part of your dream

Marilyn: Why mom?

Mindy: I want to see what my grandson will become..Maybe he will be the one who finds the cure for the virus

Marilyn: I just can't wait either

Colbert: Let's go Lyn..You are going to be late for your class..Fix your car and stop killing me in your dreams

Marilyn: C'mon dad..You know I love you..I can't wait for part two of this dream.

_To be continued!!

-It was a pleasure to have you with me during this journey into that dream..Stay tune for part two..I guarantee you it will be as fun as part one.

Thank You!!

Phito Polycarpe

www.ingramcontent.com/pod-product-compliance
Lightning Source LLC
Chambersburg PA
CBHW060246290526
45789CB00001B/219